Where Stands A Wingèd Sentry

Also published by Handheld Press

Where Stands A Wingèd Sentry

by Margaret Kennedy

Handheld Press

Handheld Classic 20

This edition published in 2021 by Handheld Press
72 Warminster Road, Bath BA2 6RU, United Kingdom.
www.handheldpress.co.uk

ISBN 978-1-912766-38-3

2 3 4 5 6 7 8 9 0

Series design by Nadja Guggi and typeset in Adobe Caslon Pro
and Open Sans.

Printed and bound in Great Britain by Short Run Press, Exeter.

FSC
www.fsc.org
MIX
Paper from
responsible sources
FSC® C014540

Contents

Faye Hammill is Professor of English Literature at the University of Glasgow. Her specialist areas are modernism and the middlebrow, periodical studies, and Canadian literature. She is author or co-author of six books, most recently *Modernism's Print Cultures* (2016), with Mark Hussey; *Magazines, Travel, and Middlebrow Culture* (2015), with Michelle Smith; and *Sophistication: A Literary and Cultural History* (2010). She has recently edited Martha Ostenso's novel *The Young May Moon* for Borealis Press (2021). She is founder of the AHRC Middlebrow Network.

Introduction

BY FAYE HAMMILL

During the summer of 1940, Britain was expecting invasion by Germany. It suddenly seemed possible that Hitler might win the war. Bombardment was anticipated in the major cities, and Margaret Kennedy was among many who hurriedly left the south-east of England, moving with her children to Cornwall. Her journal of the terrifying months from May to September 1940 was published the following year by Yale University Press and is now brought back into print for the first time.

Where Stands A Wingèd Sentry tells of a period of intense uncertainty, when ordinary life was transformed – not only by government restrictions but also by the pervasive fear of an invisible enemy. As I write this introduction, during the summer of 2020, the parallels with our contemporary experience of a pandemic are continually present to my mind. Kennedy's diary entries, with their plain style, astute political analysis, and unexpected humour, are compelling, and the book has an enormous power of immediacy. While the text was being written, and later typed out and sent to the US for safekeeping, its author still did not know whether the invasion would happen, nor whether the Allies would be victorious.

At the time when she wrote her wartime journal, Margaret Kennedy had been a celebrity for more than fifteen years, ever since the publication, when she was 28, of her novel *The Constant Nymph* (1924). A story of doomed love between a brilliant but moody composer and a fourteen-year-old girl, the book was admired by intellectuals from Thomas Hardy to Antonio Gramsci. It also became a major bestseller, and inspired stage and film versions starring Noël Coward, John Gielgud and Ivor Novello. Owing to the exceptional popular and critical success of *The Constant Nymph*, Kennedy is forever associated with the romantic atmosphere of the twenties and with the bohemian milieu that she depicted in the novel. Few readers are aware of her later work or of her important achievements in drama and non-fiction, and hardly anyone would think of her as a war writer. Yet *Where Stands A Wingèd Sentry* demonstrates that she was one, and an excellent one. She wrote, not of the London Blitz nor of factory work or hospital nursing, but of that rarely described period when Britain was getting ready for full-scale war. As the *New York Herald Tribune*'s reviewer commented: 'For the first time … some one who lived through it tells us now what happened to the English between the surrender of the Belgian army and the full force of heavy bombing. What happened was transformation' (Becker 1941, 3). Kennedy examines how the events of that phase of the conflict worked on her mind and on those of her neighbours: her book is an extraordinary record of what she describes as 'an inner battle'.

'More in the girl than meets the eye'

Margaret Kennedy's mother, Elinor Marwood, was from Yorkshire, and her father, Charles Moore Kennedy, was of Anglo-Irish heritage. Margaret, eldest of their four children, was born in 1896 in London, where Charles worked as a barrister. The household was a prosperous one. The family had access to the cultural resources of the capital as well as to the scenery of Cornwall, where they spent summer holidays (and where Elinor and Charles later settled for a time). Margaret Kennedy had a favoured education, attending Cheltenham Ladies' College and, from 1915, Somerville College, Oxford, where she was a student alongside Vera Brittain, Winifred Holtby, Naomi Mitchison and Sylvia Thompson. In a 1928 essay about this generation of women students, Holtby remembered Kennedy in this way:

> Down the street, carrying a pile of books, a kettle, and a bicycle pump, comes a woman student in a dark green

coat and a rather limp Liberty scarf. Her hat is well on the back of her head, revealing an oddly-shaped face, with an intelligent nose and quietly observant eyes. She is an unobtrusive sort of person. Apart from two or three friends, she speaks to few people; but now and then at a college debate or during a dinner-time discussion, she suddenly opens her mouth and makes about three remarks, so witty, so disconcerting and so shrewd that College pricks up its ears and wonders whether perhaps there is more in the girl than meets the eye. 'Rather a brain at history. I expect she'll go down and write a text book', said Rumour. (GREC [Holtby] 1928, 1271)[1]

And she did. Kennedy's first book, published in 1922, was *A Century of Revolution, 1789–1920*. Her career as a fiction writer began with *The Ladies of Lyndon* (1923), which is set in the Edwardian era and interweaves the stories of two main characters. Agatha is a debutante who makes a brilliant marriage and becomes mistress of Lyndon, a beautiful country house, but always regrets the loss of her first love. James, her brother-in-law, a painter of genius, is treated as a half-wit by the family but achieves happiness through his surprising marriage to a housemaid. A highly accomplished piece of work, *The Ladies of Lyndon* was well received but did not attract a large readership until after Kennedy's second novel, *The Constant Nymph*, had appeared.

The Constant Nymph, too, is set before the First World War, and centres on the eccentric Sanger family, who are remote from ordinary life in many senses. Living in an inaccessible Alpine chalet, the Sangers and their assorted houseguests are wholly absorbed by music and by a series of fantastical quarrels and romances among themselves. When the household is broken up, the young Sangers struggle to adapt to the modern world, with consequences that are initially comic but ultimately disastrous. Some readers noticed similarities between the Sanger household and the domestic set-up of Augustus John, who established an artists' colony in Dorset in 1911 and lived there with his mistress, his legitimate and his illegitimate children, and numerous long-term guests. This is plausible, since Kennedy was slightly acquainted with another painter, Henry Lamb, who had lived for a time at the Dorset colony. However, the fictional Albert Sanger can by no means be identified with a single real-life model. He is, rather, an embodiment of the idea of genius.

The Constant Nymph is about genius, and it was itself repeatedly hailed as a work of genius. Among its high-profile admirers, several of whom wrote to congratulate Kennedy or to request to meet her, were John Galsworthy, Thomas Hardy, J M Barrie, Cyril Connolly, A A Milne, George Moore, A E Housman, Walter de la Mare, William Gerhardie, Jean Giradoux, Antonio Gramsci, L P Hartley, Heywood Broun and Augustine Birrell. It is intriguing that these are all men: indeed, the novel was placed in a tradition of male-authored fiction, and numerous reviewers expressed surprise that it should have been written by a woman. It was, apparently, difficult for contemporary commentators to reconcile 'genius' with female authorship. And the themes of *The Constant Nymph* are not those that were expected in a 'woman's novel' of the period. There are no scenes of comfortable domesticity; rather, Kennedy takes up debates about art and culture. She does not shrink from the investigation of unconventional sexuality, and refuses her heroine a happy ending.

The Constant Nymph received most of its serious tributes during the first few weeks after its publication, while sales remained modest. Soon, the appeal of the novel crossed the Atlantic and, somewhat belatedly, it reached the bestseller lists. By October 1926, it was reportedly selling a thousand copies a day in the US. Its huge readership, and its successful adaptation for stage and screen, turned the book into a cultural phenomenon and Margaret Kennedy into a household name.[2]

Numerous magazines and newspapers published profiles of Kennedy, and most of these constructed her as an accidental celebrity: an ordinary woman who, in spite of her growing public reputation, had retained an appropriate feminine modesty. Some of the journalists commented on Kennedy's unexpectedly tidy and elegant appearance, which contrasted so strikingly with the outlandish styles worn by the heroine of her novel. Indeed, Kennedy did not pursue a Bohemian lifestyle, although during the early 1920s she did establish herself independently in London – much to the dismay of her more conservative relations – and *The Constant Nymph* was written in a bed-sit. However, the year after the novel appeared, Kennedy returned to a more conventionally domestic existence when she married David Davies, a barrister, who would later become Sir David Davies QC. They lived mainly in Kensington, and had two daughters, Julia (in adult life, the novelist Julia Birley) and Sally, and a son, James. (These family members feature in *Where Stands A Wingèd Sentry* under different names.) After her marriage, Kennedy continued to publish under her maiden name, which had been made so famous by her bestseller.

The Ladies of Lyndon and *The Constant Nymph* were followed by fourteen more novels. Kennedy also wrote several plays, as well as screenplays, novellas, a biography, and essays on film and fiction. Chronologically, her novels fall into two groups: those published between 1923 and 1938, and a second set, produced from 1950 onwards. Thematically, there is no clear distinction between these two waves of fictional production. She was adept at historical fiction, but also wrote contemporary stories about topics such as celebrity (*Return I Dare Not*, 1931) and divorce (*Together and Apart*, 1936). Her settings range from a Cornish seaside hotel (*The Feast*, 1950) to a Greek island (*The Forgotten Smile*, 1961), and artists, musicians and writers feature frequently in her work, as they did in her social life. Although Kennedy's readership was at its largest during the interwar years, she continued to garner respect and admiration in later decades. Her novels of the 1950s received numerous accolades: *Troy Chimneys* (1952), set during the Regency, won the James Tait Black Memorial Prize, while *The Feast* was a Literary Guild choice and *Lucy Carmichael* (1951) a Book Society selection. Over subsequent decades, her best-known work has remained in print, and in 2014 several of her novels were reissued. She has, however, attracted barely any attention from academic critics.[3]

Since Kennedy did not write fiction during the 1940s, this period has often been seen as an hiatus in her career. However, she continued to develop her dramatic and non-fiction writing during this period, producing some of her most fascinating but least known texts. Alongside *Where Stands A Wingèd Sentry*, her works of the forties include an insightful essay on contemporary cinema, *The Mechanized Muse* (1942)[4] and several plays, some of them original and others adapted from her novels. The plays did well: for instance, *How Happy With Either* ran at the St James Theatre, London in 1948, starring Constance Cummings and directed by Basil Dean, and was discussed on the 'Theatre Programme' on BBC radio ('Friday'). This was just one among many occasions during the Forties when Kennedy or her work featured on the BBC. For example, she was interviewed for the television show *Kaleidoscope* and for *Woman's Hour* on the Light Programme; both *The Constant Nymph* and *The Feast* ran as *Woman's Hour* serials; and her plays *Escape Me Never!* (1934) and *The Constant Nymph* (1926, with Basil Dean) were also broadcast on the Light Programme.[5]

Basil Dean, the influential theatre and film producer and director, was an important figure in Kennedy's career. He had persuaded her to adapt *The Constant Nymph* as a play with his help in 1926, and its success engendered Kennedy's enduring interest in writing for stage and screen. During their early attempts to write together, she was annoyed by his attributing her ideas and achievements to 'instinct', as if, as she said in a private letter, 'any mental effort on my part must be involuntary'. But a few months later, once she had watched him in action as a director, she wrote to the same friend: 'my feelings about Dean underwent an enormous change when I saw him on what is really his job'.[6] Dean later worked on both the silent (1928) and the sound (1933) film versions of *The Constant Nymph*, and on other projects with Kennedy, such as the 1937 production of her co-authored play *Autumn*.

During the 1930s and 1940s, she received commissions to work on screenplays: for instance, for *Little Friend* (1934), *The Old Curiosity Shop* (1934) and *The Man in Grey* (1943). In the same period, several of her own novels and plays were turned into films: among them, *Escape Me Never!* in 1935, and *The Midas Touch* in 1940. With at least 25 film credits to her name, Kennedy made a notable contribution to the cinema of the period. At the time when she wrote her journal of the early phase of the Second World War, Kennedy was by no means experiencing a fallow period in her career; rather, she was becoming increasingly well-known via the new media of the period.

Where Stands A Wingèd Sentry: Living Through History

In 1937, Kennedy contributed an essay to a collection in which ten novelists give the 'biographies' of their most successful books, explaining where their inspiration came from and how the writing process unfolded. In her account of the genesis of *The Constant Nymph*, Kennedy comments on the necessary time lapse between seeing a real scene and transforming it into fiction. 'Nothing is easier than to "report" – to put characters, scenes, and experiences straight into a book, to describe them in the manner of the good journalist', she claims, adding: 'Reported material can be striking and effective; skilfully faked it may even produce a temporary illusion of truth. But it can have no artistic merit whatsoever, no beauty, and its truth is too superficial to stand the test of time' (Kennedy 1937, 42). Three years later, *Where Stands A Wingèd Sentry* disproved all of this. It consists of reported material and yet it is a very powerful narrative, beautifully written and certainly of enduring significance.

Since she reached adulthood during the First World War, losing her brother in its final year, and then experienced the next war as a mother of young children, it is perhaps surprising that none of Kennedy's fiction is set against a backdrop of international conflict. Indeed, her novels perhaps tend towards escapism in their themes and atmosphere. But this makes *Where Stands a Wingèd Sentry* all the more distinctive, as an achievement in an entirely different mode. She had long kept a diary, but in spite of her literary fame had never intended it for publication. It is interesting to find that her wartime journal makes not a single mention of her literary career. She features in the narrative purely as a wife and mother and a British citizen.

In the opening entries, written in Surrey, Kennedy records the rapid alterations taking place around her – the installation of road-blocks, removal of signage and building of shelters. The sense of unreality is heightened because, at home, she is still surrounded by the comfortable appurtenances of her usual existence:

> Miss Chapman, a visiting dressmaker who has come to put our wardrobes in order ... asked when she could fit my black dinner dress which needs to be taken in. I wonder if it is worth bothering. I have an idea I shan't wear it this summer. In fact I wonder if I shall ever wear it again. (17)

The journal evokes a growing sense that whatever is about to happen will be so momentous that there will be no chance of life returning to normal afterwards. Formal dinners will likely disappear, along with the servants who make them possible. Kennedy relishes the idea of no longer having maids, since hers 'disapprove of everything I do and give me notice because they have seen me strolling down Oxford Street licking a penny ice cone, which no "gentry" would do.' After the war, she predicts, 'there won't be any more gentry, and I shall be able to walk down Oxford Street licking anything I like. If Oxford Street is still there' (53). Kennedy's habitual sense of the comic potential of everyday scenes is always inflected, in this book, with foreboding. She simultaneously fears, and welcomes, the war's potential upending of the social order.

When it became necessary to leave for the south-west, Kennedy took no maids with her, and managed her housekeeping alone while her husband remained in London. One of her entries is written in the station waiting room, just after she has said goodbye to him:

> I have an actual, physical pain in my chest as if my heart had been torn out of my body. I wonder if it would hurt as much if it had been the children I was leaving. I wonder just how many millions of women in the world have this pain now because war has parted them from their husbands. But David is right. The mother of a child as young as Charles should stay with him as long as there is any chance of invasion. (53)

As so often in this narrative, two strong instincts are in conflict with one another. Kennedy works through this conflict by a process of internal questioning and logic, just as she works through her uncertain feelings about the international situation through discussion with others and – via the diary – with herself. For instance, her attitude towards France is particularly complex. She reports the opinion of an acquaintance who claims that German propaganda has taken root in France, and that the French are not going to put up a fight. 'All this is simply frightful and I do hope her informant is an alarmist', writes Kennedy. 'Still, if I am honest, I must admit to myself that I have been stifling qualms for months and years about the French' (38). After outlining her reasons – including the allegation that they refused to pay taxes – she then considers the case for the defence: 'But then they had a far heavier measure of conscription than we had' (38). There is a pattern of advance and retreat in Kennedy's commentary on the group characteristics of different nations and social classes; she tests out positions – many of which might strike us as racist or classist now – but often ends up rejecting or modifying them. Her discussion of current political sentiment in France is pursued through an extended dialogue with her friend Jacynth, reported in detail in the diary, and this in turn ends in a comic scene which defuses the tension between them.

A diary is usually considered a transcription of the self, but Kennedy so frequently incorporates the voices of others into her entries that they take on, instead, the quality of a debate. She quotes the comments of friends with political opinions different from her own, wondering which of them is in the right. She transcribes the speech of her neighbours, her servants and her children: sometimes with humorous intent, but never dismissively. Her small daughter writes on a postcard to a school friend: 'The waw is getting very bad and we are lerning to nit'. Kennedy comments: 'if you think of it as the waw it does not seem so frightening somehow' (32). Yet the comfort she finds in her children's resilience is always tempered by fear for their safety, and at one point she even wishes that she had never brought them into the world: 'If Hitler wins they had much better be dead' (89). Another, less privileged, child who figures in the diary is 'Pearl, a little servant, a regular alley-cat of a girl from a terribly poor slum home' (35). Pearl, on hearing of Hitler's boast that he would be in London by August 15, comments: 'Eh! The cheeky monkey!' (35). Kennedy is cheered by this unsuggestibility. It helps her to believe that the British population might be able to cope with bombs if they can avoid succumbing to a belief in Hitler as invincible, or a superman: 'We must remember that monkeys have always had this habit of getting up aloft and dropping things on the heads of their betters' (35).

Down in Cornwall, Kennedy continues to observe the behaviour of adults and children from different social classes. She chose to live in St Ives, a place so familiar to her from her girlhood that she sometimes referred to it as 'my home town'.[7] In the published journal, the town is renamed Porthmerryn, but it is still easily identified since she retains the real names of Upalong, Downalong and the Artists for the main residential districts. Kennedy prefers the 'vividly alive' Downalong to the 'genteel' Upalong, and notices that the residents of the former, though they are the less prosperous group, are far more welcoming to the children who are evacuated to the town. Kennedy was reassured by the arrival of 800 evacuees in St Ives since this proved that the government considered the town a safe place. In reality, it might have been a strategic target. Joachim Von Ribbentrop, Hitler's foreign minister, made several visits there during the late 1930s, and some historians argue that the information he gathered there formed part of the German plan for invasion, and that St Ives was a possible landing site.

The last section of *Where Stands A Wingèd Sentry* contains entries from September 1940, the first one beginning: 'It has come at last'. The bombardment of London had started. As Kennedy notes: 'This is what we have been waiting for, ever since the war began. Ever since Munich. *Ever since Guernica*' (151, emphasis in the original). Yet her daily life in Cornwall remains much the same: there is still nothing she can do but wait. The journal entries pick up pace, becoming daily instead of occasional, as Kennedy awaits news of her husband and wonders whether their London house would be destroyed by a bomb (it would be, though not until 1944). In the final entry, she observes that during the past summer, 'we have certainly taken life to pieces and found out what it is made of' (179). The story ends on a note of continued uncertainty and ongoing dread, yet there is a new sense of hope and determination. Neither Kennedy nor anyone around her knows what is going to happen, yet, she says, 'I feel a force generating a resolution which is simply terrific' (169). In the book's Foreword, written in 1941, Kennedy comments that during the previous year:

> we in this country were living through a supreme experience: supreme in the collective life which is our history and supreme in our individual lives. Many of us were more frightened than we had ever expected to be. Many, before the year was out, found themselves being

braver than they had ever expected to be. We discovered unsuspected passions and loyalties. We realised which things we valued most. (3)

The collective nature of the experience – the fact that all are subject to the same regulations and the same threats, even though their responses to them are varied – is emphasised throughout. 'We all find it difficult to sleep, these days', she writes, adding: 'I expect we shall learn how to, in time, when we have got used to living through history' (49–50). This is where the real connection with our contemporary moment lies. The pandemic lockdown is not really much like the Blitz, though contemporary comparisons have been frequent. But we are certainly living through history. *Where Stands A Wingèd Sentry* demonstrates that these summer months in 2020 do have similarities to the anxious period eighty years ago when daily life changed so dramatically, and when British people began to move about, to work, and to relate to one another, in new and unprecedented ways.

Publication and reception

The 1941 Foreword gives a bulletin from a later moment in the war, and it is not the only part of the text to do this. There are also some insertions, set in italic, which Kennedy added in while she was typing up a copy of the journal. In some ways, these are reassuring, since they tell the reader that no-one in the family was killed during the events described in the 1940 entries. Yet the interpolated entries also confirm that much of what they feared in 1940 did indeed come to pass. One of the entries reads:

> *(January 25, 1941, 10.30 P.M. It's queer to think of those quiet July days now, while I am typing this out to send to the USA for safekeeping. Something very noisy is going on, and the house keeps waving about. The children are on a mattress under the kitchen table. ... Lord Halifax has arrived in USA ... And*

we are still waiting for this here invasion. But this is not an
'experiment in time' so I had better go back to July 1940.) (105)

Kennedy says in the opening section of her journal that she has written it for the benefit of her great-grandchildren. However, the effort that she went to in typing a copy and sending it overseas suggests that she saw the document as having historical and public, rather than merely personal, significance. The friend to whom she sent it, a fellow author named Julian Leonard Street, certainly thought so. The two had never met, but had conducted an extended correspondence which had its origins in Street's admiration of Kennedy's work. Born in Chicago in 1879, Street worked as a journalist, with notable contributions in art and drama criticism, and was the author of short stories and travel books in a light-hearted, humorous mode.

Street was also an experienced editor, and in her Foreword, Kennedy thanks him for editing her journal for publication. This was not the first book in this genre which he had brought out. In 1918, a volume entitled *A Woman's Wartime Journal* by Dolly Sumner Lunt, edited and annotated by Julian Street, had been published in New York. The journal covers the years 1864 and 1865, when its author lived on a Georgia plantation through which the Union army, led by General Sherman, passed on its 'March to the Sea'. In his Introduction, Street writes:

> At the time of my visit to the plantation the world was aghast over the German invasion of Belgium, the horrors of which had but recently been fully revealed and confirmed ... What, then, I began to wonder, must life have been in this part of Georgia, when Sherman's men came by? What must it have been to the woman and the little girl living on these acres, in this very house? For though Germany's assault was upon an unoffending neutral state and was the commencement of a base war, whereas Sherman's March through Georgia was an invasion of what was then

the enemy's country for the purpose of 'breaking the back' of that enemy and thus terminating the war, nevertheless 'military necessity' was the excuse in either case for a campaign of deliberate destruction. (Street 1918 viii–ix, ellipsis in original)

Street's interest in a woman's response to conflict must have been piqued, once again, by Kennedy's manuscript, which has several similarities to Lunt's. Both women debate with themselves as to the rights and wrongs of the war itself, combining this with records of anticipated and actual assaults on domestic life and property, and Kennedy refers to Lunt's work in her memoir (176).

The most powerful parts of each narrative focus on fear, physical danger and separation from family members. At the same time, both Kennedy and Lunt write in evocative terms of the loss of the treasured possessions which they used to make their houses into homes. Lunt describes herself and her neighbours burying china and silver, only to have it dug up again and smashed by the soldiers. In the September entries in her journal, Kennedy records that the plate and linen from her London house in in storage, but that if the property is bombed, 'I shall mind most about my dining-room chairs' (164). The detailed description of these cherished chairs points to the affective potential of objects, and reminds us of the special importance of material culture to a generation of women who were brought up to be, above all, home-makers. Kennedy also loved those chairs for the creative effort she had put into designing and working their covers. They were exhibited in the Empire Needlework Exhibition in 1939. Kennedy, though, was educated to a far higher level than most of her female contemporaries, and her journal demonstrates an unusually wide range of interests. A couple of pages after her entry about the dining-room chairs, she is discussing the Munich crisis. Next, she narrates a conversation about floor polish, held with a woman whom she had met on the beach and invited to her rented house for tea. Their conversation is made poignant by the revelation that this woman has lost her home in the bombing. A few pages further on, Kennedy moves to the subject of emigration to America. It was perhaps the combination of this rich content with a plain directness of style which convinced Street of the journal's potential for publication.

The letters Street sent to Kennedy before the war had a considerable influence on the content of *Where Stands A Wingèd Sentry*.[8] He told her a great deal about contemporary America and its attitudes, and she reflects frequently on this theme, and on the contrasts and connections between Britain and the US. The published journal, indeed, is explicitly addressed to an American audience. In her 1941 Foreword, she observes: 'America was constantly in my thoughts last summer. But I was thinking then of *her* future as the sole surviving democracy, the sole trustee of the Rights of Man, if we should succumb.' She adds: 'I felt a desperate ... anxiety lest the American people might repeat our mistakes' (6). Kennedy hoped that the journal might aid mutual comprehension between Americans and British, for whom, she suggests, a common language brings its own risk, that of assuming that the two peoples understand one another better than they really do.

The importance of *Where Stands A Wingèd Sentry* was immediately recognised by the American literary world. In Kennedy's archive at Somerville College, there is a typed extract from a letter written by Dorothy Canfield Fisher, an influential member of the Book-of-the-Month Club's selection committee, to Julian Street. Enclosing the text of her review, to be published in the *Book-of-the-Month Club News*, Fisher invites Street to use it for publicity purposes. (It was quoted from on the back cover flap of the published volume.) She comments: 'It would be an honor to be able to help this grand book to a wider distribution.' The obvious way to guarantee a large readership for *Where Stands A Wingèd Sentry* would have been to select it as a Book-of-the-Month. Fisher explains, however, that she was not recommending it to the committee since this would entail delaying publication for about three months after selection, a dangerous move given that the wartime situation was changing so fast. This comment reveals Fisher's belief in the book's potential to intervene, to have a tangible impact in the world.[9]

The book was, however, published by Yale University Press (where Street had connections) rather than by a trade publisher, and whilst this enhanced its intellectual prestige, it also restricted sales. *Where Stands A Wingèd Sentry* was the only one of Kennedy's books that was never published in Britain, and consequently, it was reviewed only in American periodicals. It was, though, uniformly well received. More than one reviewer objected to the title, since its source, Henry Vaughan's poem 'Peace', was not easily recognised and was thought to be 'pretentious' (Editorial 1941). But there were few other criticisms, and a large amount of praise. Many reviewers commented on the book's 'insight and integrity', as the *New York Times* put it (Woods 1941), and on Kennedy's avoidance of dramatics and hyperbole. Her style was much admired: the book is 'exquisitely and sparingly written', according to one columnist (Gannett). Reviews often dwelt on Kennedy's narrative of individual and national awakening. *The New Yorker*, for instance, wrote:

> During those four months in which England, drugged by Chamberlain, at last awoke to its danger, Miss Kennedy too awoke to certain elements in her character of which she had not been aware. The war, for all its horror, functioned as an instrument of self-discovery. And that self-discovery, she makes you feel, was no isolated personal experience. In varying forms it flowered in the minds of millions of Englishmen and Englishwomen, and from it a better England may rise. (Fadiman 72)

The reviewer is sensitive to Kennedy's strategy of alternately describing her own responses and those of the people around her, so as to build an impression of a collective mind and a shared determination. Others remarked on the way that the book supplemented and amplified more factual reporting. The

Indianapolis News commented: 'It is a kaleidoscopic picture ... really more complete than the official picture of gains and losses, for it is a picture of English morale' ('The New Books'). Indeed, 'morale' is a repeated term across the reviews. Kennedy's narrative avoids the jingoism and sentiment of many overtly morale-boosting wartime texts, speeches and broadcasts. Yet its capacity to influence and to inspire was very widely recognised in 1941, and will be appreciated anew by twenty-first-century readers.

Notes

1   For a discussion of this essay, and the accompanying illustration, see Clay 2018, 127–28.

2   See Hammill 2007, 124–151, for a detailed discussion of the reception and cultural status of the novel and its relationship to Kennedy's celebrity persona.

3   Among the works listed under 'Further Reading', those which discuss Kennedy's work are Cockburn, Hammill, Leonardi, and Melman; see also Powell's biography.

4   *The Mechanized Muse* is referred to in several books on cinema history; for recent examples see Cartmell 77; Marcus 437.

5   This information comes from the BBC's Genome Project, which provides a digital archive of issues of *The Radio Times*. https://genome.ch.bbc.co.uk/

6   Margaret Kennedy to Flora Forster. Margaret Kennedy Collection, Somerville College, Oxford, Add. mss. Box 26, SC/LY/SP/MK 26/2. Letter 31 (8 April 1926); Letter 33 (8 October 1926).

7   Margaret Kennedy to Flora Forster. Letter 17 (9 November 1924).

8   The letters are held in the Julian Street Papers, Firestone Library, Princeton University (Box 21: Davies, Margaret Kennedy) and in the Margaret Kennedy Collection, Somerville College, Oxford (Box 12: Julian Street Papers). As a consequence of the pandemic, these archives remained closed while I was preparing this Introduction. I had not consulted these letters during my previous visit to Somerville, so I cannot quote from them.

9   A typescript of the review, with an undated extract from Fisher's letter,
    is included in an envelope of clippings relating to *Where Stands A Wingèd
    Sentry* in the Margaret Kennedy Collection, Somerville College, Oxford,
    Box 11: American Reviews, SC/LY/SP/MK 11/3. My thanks to Kate O'Donnell,
    archivist, for sending these.

Works Cited

Becker, May Lamberton, 'A Silent Passion Beyond Tears and Cheers', rev. of *Where Stands a Wingèd Sentry* by Margaret Kennedy, *New York Herald Tribune Books*, 14 September 1941, XI: 3.

Cartmell, Deborah, *Screen Adaptations: Jane Austen's* Pride and Prejudice: *The Relationship Between Text and Film* (Methuen 2010).

Clay, Catherine, *Time and Tide: The Feminist and Cultural Politics of a Modern Magazine* (Edinburgh University Press 2018).

Editorial, *Medford Mail Tribune* (Oregon), 11 September 1941, 12.

Fadiman, Clifton, 'Books: England – Oysters', *The New Yorker*, 13 September 1941, 72, 74.

'Friday April 30: Light Programme', *The Radio Times*, 23 April 1948, 19.

Gannett, Lewis. 'Books and Things', *New York Herald Tribune*, 9 September 1941, 19.

GREC [Winifred Holtby), 'Parnassus in Academe: Novelists at Oxford', *Time and Tide*, 28 December 1928, 1271–72.

Hammill, Faye, *Women, Celebrity, and Literary Culture Between the Wars* (University of Texas Press 2007).

Kennedy, Margaret, '*The Constant Nymph*', in *Titles to Fame*, ed. by Denys Kilham Roberts (Thomas Nelson 1937), 21–50.

Marcus, Laura, *The Tenth Muse: Writing About Cinema in the Modernist Period* (Oxford University Press 2007).

'The New Books', *The Indianapolis News*, 11 September 1941, 6.

Street, Julian, Introduction to *A Woman's Wartime Journal* by Dolly Sumner Lunt (New York: Century, 1918), v–xi.

Woods, Katherine, 'Britain's Battle Reflected in a Woman's Journal', *New York Times*, 21 September 1941, BR9.

Further reading

Cockburn, Claud. *Bestseller: The Books That Everyone Read 1900–1939* (Sidgwick and Jackson 1972).

Ellis, Steve, *British Writers and the Approach of World War II* (Cambridge University Press 2015).

Feigel, Lara, *The Love-Charms of Bombs: Restless Lives in the Second World War* (Bloomsbury 2013).

Garfield, Simon. *We Are At War: The Diaries of Five Ordinary People in Extraordinary Times* (Ebury Press 2005).

Last, Nella. *Nella Last's War: The Second World War Diaries of Housewife, 49*, ed. by Richard Broad and Suzie Fleming (1981; Profile Books, 2006).

Leonardi, Susan J, *Dangerous by Degrees: Women at Oxford and the Somerville College Novelists* (Rutgers University Press 1989).

Melman, Billie. *Women and the Popular Imagination in the 1920s: Flappers and Nymphs* (Macmillan 1988).

Miles, Constance. *Mrs Miles's Diary: The Wartime Journal of a Housewife on the Home Front*, ed. by S V Partington (Simon and Schuster, 2013).

Morgan, Fidelis. *The Years Between: Plays by Women on the London Stage 1900–1950* (Virago 1994).

Powell, Violet. *The Constant Novelist: A Study of Margaret Kennedy, 1896–1967* (Heinemann 1983).

Works by Margaret Kennedy

Novels

The Ladies of Lyndon (Heinemann 1923)

The Constant Nymph (Heinemann 1924)

Red Sky at Morning (Heinemann 1927)

The Fool of the Family (Heinemann 1930)

Return I Dare Not (Heinemann 1931)

A Long Time Ago (Heinemann 1932)

Together and Apart (Cassell 1936)

The Midas Touch (Cassell 1938)

The Feast (Cassell 1950)

Lucy Carmichael (Macmillan 1951)

Troy Chimneys (Rinehart 1952)

The Oracles (Macmillan 1955; as *Act of God* Rinehart, 1955)

The Heroes of Clone (Macmillan 1957; as *The Wild Swan* Rinehart, 1957)

A Night in Cold Harbour (Macmillan 1960)

The Forgotten Smile (Macmillan 1961)

Not in the Calendar: The Story of a Friendship (Macmillan 1964)

Novellas

A Long Week-End (Doubleday 1927)

The Game and the Candle (Heinemann 1928)

Dewdrops (Heinemann 1928)

Women at Work (Macmillan 1966)

Plays

The Constant Nymph, with Basil Dean (Heinemann 1926)

Come With Me, with Basil Dean (Heinemann 1928)

Escape Me Never! (dramatisation of *The Fool of the Family*; Heinemann 1934)

Autumn, with Gregory Ratoff (adapted from the book by Ilya Surguchev; Nelson 1940)

The Phoenix and the Dove (dramatisation of *A Long Time Ago*; broadcast 1941)

Who Will Remember? (Dramatic Publishing Company 1946)

How Happy with Either (unpublished; performed 1948)

Non-fiction

A Century of Revolution, 1789–1920 (Methuen 1922)

Where Stands a Wingèd Sentry (Yale University Press 1941)

The Mechanized Muse (Allen & Unwin 1942)

Jane Austen (Barker 1950)

The Outlaws on Parnassus (Cresset 1958)

Kennedy's uncollected works include film scripts, short stories, and essays.

Note on the text

The text was scanned and proofread against the Yale University Press first edition of 1941. The section breaks in the original indicated with an extra line space have been made more definite by using small crosses instead, to signal the change of tone or mood that the author intended. Dialogue in French which had italics in the original has had the italics removed.

Where Stands A Wingèd Sentry

My soul, there is a country
Afar beyond the stars,
Where stands a wingèd sentry
All skillful in the wars …

—Henry Vaughan (1622–1695)

To the Memory of My Mother and Father

Foreword

May 16, 1941

A year ago today the French line was broken at Mézières. From that day until the end of the first phase of the Battle of Britain, in October, we in this country were living through a supreme experience: supreme in the collective life which is our history and supreme in our individual lives. Many of us were more frightened than we had ever expected to be. Many, before the year was out, found themselves being braver than they had ever expected to be. We discovered unsuspected passions and loyalties. We realised which things we valued most.

The collapse of France was so much more than a mere material blow, the loss of a military ally, the weakening of our strategic resources. It was the collapse of part of our faith. It bewildered us, as if the bottom had fallen out of the world. It made the forces of Evil seem immeasurably strong. Only after several months did we begin to understand a little how such a tragedy had come about, to guess at our own share in the mistakes which had been made, to realise how

> For superior energies; most strict
> Affiance in each other; faith more firm
> In their unhallowed principles; the bad
> Have fairly earned a victory o'er the weak,
> The vacillating, inconsistent good.

This was cold comfort, but it did show a way out of a nightmare. Such a perspective does at least put energy, faith, and loyalty back where we have always known they ought to be, and does suggest that the final victory will go to that side which makes the best use of these virtues. If the Good, and I make no apology for so describing all freedom-loving peoples, will now take example by the Bad in this respect, they may still win a war which, by their own fault, they nearly lost in 1940.

There was a time in the summer of 1940 when it almost seemed as if sheer badness was a dominant principle. The landmarks we most trusted vanished suddenly. A sense of deadly peril weighed upon us, but far worse was the fog of falsity, of betrayal, spreading all over the world its weary, bitter disgust and doubt. For some months it seemed as if we had to travel quite alone, and that the nations of the world, like the hostile hills surrounding the Dark Tower, thronged with dead men, were watching silently, coldly, to see the last of us.

We do not know what happened to Childe Roland when he blew his horn and summoned the Thing from the Dark Tower. We do know what happened when we blew our challenge. The battle is scarcely joined yet and the hardest part of it is yet to be endured. But the evil spell is no longer upon us, and we are fighting, not in a fog of illusion, but in the light of common day. And we know that we are not alone; all freedom-loving men in the world are with us. Many are able to help in material ways. All give us their prayers.

The story of last summer is the story of forty million people, each one of them taking that journey. Each had to find his own path back to faith and sanity, each had his own unuttered fears, each found his own sources of courage. If each one were to write his own account of it no two stories would be quite alike. Many, perhaps too many, books have been written about bombs and shelters. One bomb sounds pretty much like another. But of the four months when we were all getting mentally ready for the bombs not so much has been said. Only now are we ourselves beginning to speak to one another of that inner battle – a sign of our certainty that this part of our ordeal is over.

My own account of it was not originally written for publication. It forms part of a journal which I have kept for years. Last autumn I made a separate book out of the period May-September, and sent a copy to the United States for safekeeping. Now that parts of it are to be published, there are one or two things which I think I should say to American readers.

I have, in the first place, changed the names of places and people referred to. I have done this because it is what I would wish others to do to me in like case. I detest finding myself mentioned by name in somebody else's book. The people mentioned here may recognise themselves and remember the occasions described, but they don't have to feel that I have caught them in an unguarded moment and exhibited them by name to the world, like a candid camera man.

Secondly, I ought to amend the statement I made in the prefatory chapter I wrote last autumn – that a life that is very nearly normal is still being led in many parts of this island. Nor is my description of Porthmerryn in June, 1940, at all accurate today. There are now, I should imagine, very few places in England or Scotland which do not know what a bomb sounds like, though life is still more normal in the country than in the towns. Nor should anyone suppose that we are still eating cream. We are not now eating too much of anything, though we still get enough of all essentials to keep us healthy.

We in Porthmerryn have got the sea on our doorstep. Visitors who come here for a short rest from life in the big cities are shocked at sights to which we have grown accustomed: the lifeboat going out day after day, the ambulance waiting at the jetty, the sombre little parties of fishermen carrying a coffin up to the graveyard on the hill, the many flags which drape those coffins, Dutch, Belgian, Norwegian, Free French,

British. Every high tide brings us some token of what is going on out there, and we don't let the children play alone on the rocks any more for fear of what they might find. The toll of Porthmerryn men is high, as it was in the last war.

I would like, also, to remind American readers that this journal was written before the Lease-Lend Bill was so much as dreamt of, before Mr Wilkie was nominated as a presidential candidate. Most of it was written at a time when it seemed likely that the United States would move in the direction of stricter isolation rather than of increased aid to Britain. It may seem as if some of my references to America are rather detached, almost ungrateful, unless this is remembered. It must be as difficult for Americans to think themselves back into last year as it is for us; but anyone who can do so must admit that I would have been guilty of very rash and wishful thinking if I had ever assumed that cooperation between our two countries would go as far and as fast as it has done.

America was constantly in my thoughts last summer. But I was thinking then of her future as the sole surviving democracy, the sole trustee of the Rights of Man, if we should succumb. (Which is what she well might have been, by now, if it had not been for the RAF.) I felt a desperate need to be sure that liberty would survive somewhere, and anxiety lest the American people might repeat our mistakes and fail to arm themselves in time or fail to guard against internal espionage.

Finally, I want to express my deep gratitude to Julian Street, who has edited this journal for publication. Not only do I thank him for his kindness to me, but for all that he and his wife are doing, and have done, for my countrymen in their bitter struggle. His letters to me, even in the darkest days, were so full of humanity and sane cheerfulness that they always gave me heart. He told me many things about America and American opinion which it is good that we should know over here. It was one of the great tragedies of the last war that the Americans and the British fought and died together without really fully understanding one another's point of view. We each believed that the other was fighting for 'democracy' without taking into account the different meanings which can be attached to that word. Men of good will, anxious to promote a good understanding between our countries, tried to ignore those criticisms which must always exist between two proud nations, instead of admitting them and examining them in a friendly and constructive spirit.

I think public opinion in both countries is much better informed today than it was twenty years ago. We know more about one another. The radio has done much to help this. I know of no household which does not listen to 'American Commentary' regularly. Had there been anything like it in the last war I do not think we should have come to such grief over the peace.

The common language is a great help but it is also to some degree a danger. We should be continually astonished and delighted at the number of things we have in common, if we had the barrier of language to overcome, but speaking the same tongue we are often tempted to suppose that we understand one another better than we do, and it is the unsuspected differences which surprise and irritate us.

Mr Street's letters have done much to explain America to me. And even in the worst days they calmed my fears. For they strengthened my certainty that, whatever policy America might decide to pursue, she would never allow herself to be tricked or intimidated, and that, whatever happened to us, freedom would have a good chance of surviving under the American flag. I needed to know that much more than I needed to know what guns, tanks, and planes she was likely to send us.

Chapter One

Talthybius Speaking

All my life I have had a great curiosity to know what it felt like to live through history. I have wondered how ordinary, everyday people, like myself, felt and thought while they were waiting for the news of Waterloo, or when they saw the beacon fires which told them the Armada had sailed. Were they horribly frightened or were they always quite sure they would win? Did they realise all that was at stake or did the little commonplaces of life still hold the foreground in their minds? Could they sleep and, if they slept, what kind of dreams did they have? What kind of jokes sustained them and what sort of prayers did they say?

Lately I have lived through history myself – quite a bit of history. So I have written an account of it, while it is still fresh in my mind, for the benefit of my great-grandchildren. Most of the memoir is transcribed from a journal which I kept. It contains few dates and little that will be found in history books. It is simply a record of what I have myself seen, heard, thought, and felt, from day to day.

My great-grandchildren will probably be surprised to find so few bombs in this memoir. There are still many people in England who have never seen or heard a bomb, and there are some who have never even heard a siren. A life that is nearly normal is still being led in many parts of this island, and I think that records of this semi-normal life will be far rarer, in the future, than stories of life in the London shelters.

✳

My story begins at six o'clock on an evening in May, 1940, when the BBC announcer told the British people that the situation of our army in Flanders was one of 'ever-increasing gravity'.

Those three words banished for ever the comfortable delusion that we were 'certain to win'. And, from that moment, the war took on a new character in our minds. We had met with shocks and disappointments, we had become increasingly conscious of muddle and lost opportunities, of the necessity for greater exertion and sterner sacrifice. But we had never doubted the issue. Setbacks were deplored as merely delaying the day of success. We had believed that Hitler could not win, that time was on our side, and that we had plenty of time. All but a very few of us believed that. The idea that we could possibly be beaten was something for which our minds were totally unprepared. It took our breath away. Never before in all its history has this nation been so profoundly and unanimously shocked as it was on that evening in May.

✕

We were living at that time in Surrey. Our London house was being used as a warden's post. Our household consisted of my mother-in-law, her nurse companion, our three children, Ellen, aged twelve, Lucy, aged ten, and Charles, aged five, Miss Wright, the governess, old Nanny, a cook, a housemaid, a parlour-maid, David, and myself. We also had with us Claire, the eleven-year-old daughter of friends, who had been put in my care for the duration. David went to work every day in London, but he usually managed to get down to Surrey in the evenings and at weekends.

I shall begin at the moment when Miss Wright and I were sitting on the sofa in the drawing room of the Surrey house, listening to that awful news bulletin. But before I do so I think I had better say a few words about the BBC news bulletins which may explain why it was such a shock to us. Because it might be difficult for anyone who had not heard them, during the early months of the war, to understand how we came to be so mutton-headed.

✕

In Greek tragedy there is a character called Talthybius whose role it is to break bad news to the Protagonists. He tells about lost battles, sacked cities, and murdered children. And he makes a fine art of it, spinning out his dreadful tale as long as possible and keeping everybody in suspense. Often, just to make it all more difficult, he is deliberately cryptic, and keeps on saying things which have a double meaning.

Our modern Talthybius, the BBC announcer, has something of the same technique. It is not always easy to make out what he is really saying. The more significant items of news are often artfully concealed in a mass of irrelevances, like sixpences in a pudding. They don't always come first on the list and unless we listen closely we are liable to miss them.

> This is the BBC Home Service. Here is the news. The butter ration is to be increased. The Prime Minister has spoken on War Savings. Amiens and Arras have been occupied by the enemy. There is good news for pig farmers. Fifteen French generals have been relieved of their commands. At the end of the news Mr X will speak about the prospects of homegrown sugar beet.

This is scarcely a caricature of the sort of thing that has been served up to us.

People who happen to look at maps, who realise that Amiens is probably the supply base for the BEF, who remember its importance during the last war, who have read enough history to realise what the dismissal of fifteen generals probably implies, those people may feel slightly sick at this list of news items. But most of us don't look at maps, have not studied history, and remember very little about the last war except that our side won after apparently losing a great many battles. There is nothing in the manner of the announcer to suggest that anything of vital importance has been said. Among millions, the first reaction to such a bulletin would be:

'Good! More butter. *They* seem to have got two more French towns which is bad, but the French are getting a lot of new generals, so perhaps things will go better.'

I don't know who writes the scripts for the news bulletins. Everything in them is probably quite true and accurate, but for all that the nation has been misled. Or rather, it has not been led at all. There is a great deal of difference between telling the truth and telling no lies.

Not that there has been any deliberate attempt at deception. I don't believe the Chamberlain government cared twopence what we knew or what we thought, one way or the other, and they issued news items in that spirit. We had this whim, this caprice, to know how the war was getting along, which was a great nuisance when they were all so busy, and so a few facts were flung to us at random, and we were left to make what we liked of them.

They tried to run the war in the manner of good civil servants, and nobody has a greater contempt for public opinion than a first-rate English civil servant. Perhaps it is because we are all so meek and law-abiding. We pay our taxes promptly and without grumbling, and we fill up correctly all forms sent to us and post them on the right date. Therefore they despise us, as servants despise easy-going masters, or as children despise a father who always uncomplainingly foots the bill. Hitler understands that total war cannot be waged in that manner. He does not dare to flout public opinion, but takes the greatest pains to lie to it and flatter it. But he is not a civil servant. Our civil servants take the stand that if we have no confidence in them we can oust them, since we are a democracy. *But in the meantime pray do not speak to the man at the wheel.*

So that is why we all went on so comfortably through the disastrous Norwegian campaign and through the early stages of the invasion of the Low Countries. Holland was knocked out, the French lines were dented, broken, the Battle of the Bulge became the Battle of the Gap, Gamelin went, Weygand was called in, tanks drove a wedge between the English and the French armies, Amiens and Arras fell, the Battle of the Gap became the Battle for the Ports – Abbéville, Boulogne, Calais. And it was still mixed up with soothing items about sugar beet and pig farming.

But the day of reckoning came at last.

Ever-increasing gravity. Anybody could understand that. Forty million people gasped and woke up.

Chapter Two

May: 'Ever-Increasing Gravity'

1

Miss Wright jumped visibly and gave a little squeak as if something had bitten her. I felt as if I was going down very fast in a lift. We looked at each other, each hoping that she might have heard it wrong.

After the news was over Miss Wright picked up her knitting and knitted furiously for half a row. Then she put it down again and sighed and said half under her breath:

'It makes you sick to think of. If ...'

I didn't have to ask what the 'if' meant. If Hitler can win this battle he might win the war. If he wins the war ...

I went up to see my mother-in-law. She was playing piquet with Nurse Ross. She said she was quite sure there had been a misprint in the news bulletin. She said there often is. Probably it was ever-*decreasing* gravity. Nurse Ross said they shouldn't say things like that on the wireless. It is very upsetting for people. A person with a weak heart might die of it.

I went out onto the lawn where I found Cotter, the gardener, bedding out geraniums. He too had heard the six o'clock news and he looked perturbed but not flabbergasted. But it would take the last trump to dismay Cotter, and even then he would probably appoint himself an usher and marshal us all to our places before the mercy seat. He runs the entire village, the British Legion, the Cricket Club, and the Parish Council. It's my belief that he was born giving instructions to the midwife.

According to him, Hitler is a mad bull. When it rushes you shouldn't try to stop it. You just let it rush. After a while it stops rushing and then you counter-attack.

'But supposing he doesn't stop rushing?'

'Get farther away from his base all the time,' said Cotter tolerantly.

Oh, I don't know. I don't know. That didn't seem to worry the Germans in Poland.

I wandered round the garden pulling up a few weeds in the iris bed and picking some lilacs to take in to my mother-in-law. It was a perfect evening and at least five cuckoos were shouting down in the valley woods. Never has there been such a spring for blossom. I was tense and taut and aching a little all over. I kept repeating *ever-increasing gravity* over and over again, or rather it kept repeating itself to me, as if the wireless had followed me out of the house and was haunting my footsteps everywhere.

I went through the little gate into the paddock. The three girls came cantering towards me on their ponies, Lucy shouting out to know if I would read to them. Ellen glanced at me sharply. She sees a lot with her short-sighted eyes.

'What is it, Mother? Is the war getting very bad?'

'It is rather.'

(Never show dismay in front of a child, says the *Manual for Mothers* which I have studied so conscientiously.)

Lucy grins and says:

'Poor grown-ups!'

For, as they explained to me some time ago, the worst part of a war is having to hear the grown-ups 'going on and on about it.'

'But *are* you going to read to us?'

We are reading *Penrod*, by Booth Tarkington, a book they make me read at least once a year. I don't read it very well, it always makes me laugh so much.

As I went upstairs I met Miss Chapman, a visiting dressmaker who has come to put our wardrobes in order. She asked when she could fit my black dinner dress which needs to be taken in. I wonder if it is worth bothering. I have an idea I shan't wear it this summer. In fact I wonder if I shall ever wear it again.

I found *Penrod* and went down to the girls and read to them without understanding a single word I was reading. *Ever-increasing gravity*. What does it mean? I know what it means well enough, but I can't get the idea into my head. It is like trying to wrap up a parcel in a piece of paper too small for it. I suppose we shall know more tomorrow.

2

We do indeed know more.

Belgium is out. King Leopold has capitulated. The BEF is cut off from the French on the south and now its whole northern flank is left unprotected. We have looked at the map to see what ports we have got left; Dunkirk seems to be about the only one. How can they fight their way back to Dunkirk, attacked on three sides? And how can half a million men be got away from there with all Hitler's planes bombing them as they embark?

The French are furious with Leopold and call him a traitor, and our papers are full of bitter contrasts between him and his father, and hints of sinister influences which have surrounded him. But how can we know what pressure was used, what blackmailing threats of bombing and massacre for his people? It is getting too easy to call people traitors and to imagine that they are acting from motives which are mean and base.

That is what Hitler is doing to us: he is poisoning men's minds against each other, debauching the conscience of the world, and creating everywhere a doubt of the virtues of human nature. His creed starts from the undeniable truth that men are timid, greedy, and gullible, and argues that human affairs must therefore be managed on gangster lines. Well, it is also true that men are brave, honest, and disinterested, and in a gangster world they would have no chance to develop their true natures. But the devil of it is that whenever any ruler, or any nation, fails to be completely heroic, compromises, or makes a muddle, it looks like support for Hitler's argument. Human goodness has never been so challenged before, not even by Machiavelli. Leopold is probably just like all the rest of us, a poor, wretched, terrified, bewildered human being, trying to act for the best.

But what an unspeakable calamity for us and for the Belgians! Only a fortnight ago our troops were pouring in across their frontier and the newspapers were full of pictures of the people cheering them and throwing lilac sprays into the lorries. We were going to defend Belgium.

※

It is another unbearably lovely day. I went up to the top of Holmbury Hill. You look south there for miles and miles across Surrey and Sussex, over a patchwork of little fields and smudges of woods and the red roofs of farmhouses. On the horizon is the blue line of the South Downs, and a little knob on one of them which is the clump of huge beeches called Chanctonbury Ring. And beyond them is the sea. And beyond that France. And there, under the same cloudless sky, all this hell of suffering and terror is going on at this very moment. Farms are blazing. Homeless wretches stray along the roads. Mothers howl for dead babies, and children for dead mothers. And our men are dying in this sunshine upon a soil they could not defend.

Oh, the mind cannot take in all the suffering there is in

the world. It cannot comprehend or endure it. When we try to imagine a being who could, we picture Him hanging for ever upon a cross.

✕

David came home from London this evening. He looks fagged and wretched. He was very ill with pleurisy in March and is not really fit yet to be back at work.

At supper he told us that a man got into his compartment in the train, coming down, in a state of nervous collapse. He had a perfectly green face and kept saying:

'This means we're done. We're finished. We've been licked. It's the end. We can't go on.'

At last a fat man in the corner said:

'If you must go on saying that, go and say it in the toilet.'

Nurse Ross suggested that the man was suffering from 'nairrves'. She puts down any emotional behaviour to nerves. She is a tall, rawboned, handsome Scotswoman with no interest on earth outside her job. She pays very scant attention to the war. I have the greatest difficulty in enforcing the blackout in her patient's room at night. David's mother suffers from angina and must have plenty of air. On stuffy nights Nurse Ross tears the black curtains from the windows the moment my back is turned. If I protest she says:

'Ah, she'll no need the blackoot. Ye can black oot a' the ither rooms, but ye'll no need tae fash with hers.'

When I point out that an uncurtained window makes me liable to a fine of fifty pounds, she says:

'They'll no fine ye if ye tell them we've an angina case in the hoose.'

Miss Wright suspected the man on the train of trying deliberately to create panic. We talked for a while of Fifth Column methods and the paralysing effect of suspicion and distrust in a community and how the German people are kept down by being encouraged to suspect and spy on each other. Miss Wright said finally:

'Well, anyway, whatever happens, they can't make Nazis of *us*.'

And a look of mulish obstinacy settled on her face.

David and I, mindful of Gestapo methods and Dachau, were just about to exclaim,

'Oh, *can't* they?'

But we paused and looked at her, and thought again. There was something reassuringly tough about her expression, and I believe that our nation is, as a whole, as immutable and unsuggestible as Miss Wright and Nurse Ross.

David and I are weaker vessels. I hope and trust that we would have the strength to be martyrs if it should become our duty, but we are much more rattled than Miss Wright and Nurse Ross. We have more imagination, and imagination cuts both ways. We have travelled too much. Too many of our friends are 'foreigners' and we have tried too hard to see things from the point of view of other nations. This is no doubt a good thing, but it has made us less immune from the plagues which are sweeping across the world. If you try to get near to other human beings you sometimes merely catch their colds.

We are European Liberals, a type which is terribly at a discount now. I still believe that ours is the right road to peace and freedom for all men, but we have failed for the time being, and our failure is partly due to the fact that we did not try hard enough. We did not risk all, sacrifice all to preach our creed, as many of our opponents did. We did not throw ourselves into the cause of Liberalism with the zeal and energy that the Communists and Fascists can command in their followers. We have lived too easily, enjoyed ourselves too much. A world in which everyone was as happy as David and I have been would be a wonderful place. But if we want to secure such a world we must gird ourselves for a much sterner, more strenuous existence and never in our lifetime seek repose.

✕

After supper we went for what David calls a little waddle through the dusky woods, hoping to hear a nightingale. We didn't hear one, though the cook says they have been yelling fit to deafen her all the afternoon outside her scullery window.

It was nearly dark when we turned towards home. Somewhere in the woods they were chopping down trees, although it was so late. The axe fell again and again in the quiet dusk, like a slow clock ticking:

Chop! Chop! Chop!

David said, after a long silence:

'I must remember to get my bathing suit next time I go to the London house.'

I laugh, because I know exactly how he has got to thinking of his bathing suit. The sound of the axe made him think of the play, *The Cherry Orchard*, where they begin to cut down the trees in the last act, and the curtain goes down to the sound of the axe. Thinking of Chekhov he remembered a Chekhov story, 'In the Valley', which I am always praising and which he is always saying he must read. He determined to read it now, and then remembered that all our books are in the London house. So he thought he would fish out that volume of Chekhov next time he went there, and then recollected that he wanted to collect his bathing suit as well.

After fifteen years of marriage we often pursue a conversation like this, in silence, each knowing where the other has got to.

3

O my goodness! It seems that the reason they were cutting down trees so late last night was that they were building a sort of fort of pine logs, guarding the road just outside Charles's kindergarten.

What for?

Invasion.

Cotter says they are hastily putting up log barricades on all the roads and taking down the sign-posts, and the farmers have orders to put obstructions in large fields where troop-carrying planes might be landed. The British Legion has been told to guard the local telephone exchange. There are notices in the village telling us what to do if we see parachute troops coming down. We are to lock up all cars and bicycles at night and if we leave a car unattended it must pretty well be disembowelled. Apparently it won't do just to take out the ignition key because the Germans know all about hairpins.

All these things have happened in the last twenty-four hours. So the government must really think invasion possible.

And why not? The Nazis have Norway and Holland and Denmark and Belgium, and now the French Channel ports: all the coasts facing ours. When they have mopped up the BEF in Flanders why shouldn't they invade us? We have no army here. Could the navy stop them? Hitler landed troops in Norway in spite of the navy. But that was Fifth Column work.

Is he expecting to do the same thing here? Has he got a Fifth Column here? Are there really English people who *could*?

Cotter says somebody has been coming at dead of night and putting pro-Nazi literature into the letter-box of the British Legion Club. He is very busy sleuthing the culprit and his account of his activities sounds like an Oppenheim novel. Ten to one it will turn out to be some harmless crank.

But I don't like it at all. I hate the idea of a blockhouse outside Charles's school.

4

Today we have all been to church because the King asked us to go. Every church, chapel, and meeting-house in the country has been packed during this week. If the Archbishop of Canterbury had called us to prayer I doubt if we would have turned up in such numbers. We would feel that he was merely advertising his own wares:

TRY PRAYER —
INFALLIBLE CURE FOR INEFFICIENCY

But we like the King and we are very sorry for him, as he has a stiff row to hoe. If it helps him to pray and to have us pray with him, to church we will go.

I wonder what most people prayed for. Probably, quite simply and naively, for victory. Nurse Ross said she prayed for the death of Hitler. Ellen prayed that Hitler and Mussolini might have a change of heart. Whereat Lucy observed that it is unnecessary to pray for Mussolini.

'If Hitler got pious,' she said, 'Mussolini would have to follow suit.'

But a great many people do not think it right to pray for victory, since Germans are undoubtedly praying for it too, and we might put the Lord into an awkward position. We are all His children; how then can we ask Him to take sides? There is a lot to be said for that point of view. But it must surely be all right to pray that both England and Germany may be delivered from the Nazis.

A comfortable compromise is to pray that Right may triumph and that we may be enabled to do our duty, secure in the conviction that we are right and that it is our duty to lick the Huns. Also it is quite easy to pray that God's will may be done, if you are sure that He can't want Hitler to win. And who could imagine such a thing?

A few stern moralists can. I have met people who believe that an appalling wave of suffering and persecution is needed, over the whole world, to bring mankind back to God. A Roman Catholic friend of mine holds this view. I said:

'Back to the Christian conception of God as a loving Father?'

She said this world doesn't matter, and suffering doesn't matter, and our attempts to make it a better place are too materialistic. All that matters is our salvation in the next world.

'In effect,' said I, 'the more wretched we are here below, the more ready we shall be to listen to people who tell us that there will be Pie in the Sky when we Die?'

When we have discovered a cure for cancer, a remedy for poverty, when we have disposed of all the shocks, bereavements, injustices, and cares which oppress mankind – shall we then cease to thirst for God? Is it only in hours of misery that we feel we are merely watching the shadows on the rock and that this world is not our home? Is not all bliss, all ecstasy, merely a message, an intimation of some perfect harmony that exists elsewhere? I have heard Toscanini conduct a perfect performance of the Seventh Symphony. Perfect? Merely an assurance that there must be perfection somewhere. *Hast mich in eine bessere Welt.*

✳

Nevertheless, I thought, as I hunted for my church hat, there will probably be some searchings of the heart today among people who don't pray often. Why should we clamour to God in the time of our tribulation when we failed to call upon Him in the time of our wealth? And how shall we escape from our sins? When I pray, as I can't help praying, desperately, childishly, as one who cries: Abba! Father! that Ellen and Lucy and Charles shall not be bombed, my conscience replies coldly with one word:

'Guernica.'

The Reds say the Germans did it. The Franquists say the Reds did it. What matter? A horrible crime was committed, the first of its kind in Europe. An open Spanish town, containing no military objective, was annihilated, and women and children were machine-gunned as they fled to the fields. All Europe was shocked. All Spain was shocked and each side hastened to fasten responsibility onto the other. Nobody has ever attempted to say that Guernica was not destroyed. But in England and France everybody cried out in horror and then looked away, because the delicacy of the diplomatic situation made it impossible to interfere. Most people knew in their hearts that the lid had been taken off hell, and that what had been done in Guernica would one day be done in London, Paris, and Berlin.

Supposing all those people had risen up and said, 'We won't stand this. Something has been done which defiles our civilisation. It must never be repeated. We are not interested in the right or wrongs of the Spanish Civil War. We differ among ourselves about that. But we demand that these enemies of civilisation shall be brought to justice, whichever side they are on. An international tribunal, acting in the interests of the whole world, must be set up, the evidence must be impartially examined, and when it is established who destroyed Guernica those criminals must be outlawed, be they Spaniards, Russians, Germans, or Italians.'

Impossible! There is no machinery for making the moral will of nations effective. Moral force, the conscience of the peoples, does exist and is felt; it comes into operation eventually and affects the course of history. But it seldom comes into action in time to do much good, and sometimes it does actual harm. An outburst of moral indignation in England and France wrecked the Hoare-Laval plan for the settlement of the Abyssinian question, and forced the governments of both countries to impose sanctions on Italy. Too late. Abyssinia was not saved and Italy was alienated from the democracies.

'O Heavenly Father, don't remember Guernica! You see we have not yet got democratic control of foreign policy.'

'And whose fault is that, my daughter?'

⁜

The hawthorn is so thick this year, it is like clotted cream in all the hedges. Great gusts of perfume met us as we walked in the bland sunshine across the fields to church. The path lies over the brow of a hill, past twelve huge elm trees which are a landmark for miles round and are known locally as the Twelve Apostles, and down through a little spinney to the village in the valley. The bells were ringing an oddly merry peal. Upon all the footpaths cutting across the green fields were dark clumps of people, cottage families in their Sunday clothes moving towards one centre. The cuckoos were hard at it.

Ding-dong! Cuckoo! Ding-dong! Cuckoo!

When we got out of the spinney we had a view of the triangular village green where a great many middle-aged men, farmers, labourers, and shopkeepers, were standing about while Cotter barked round them like a trusty sheep dog: the British Legion, about to parade. The Boy Scouts and the Girl Guides had already paraded and were following the Red Cross into church.

We stood aside to let them get in. The bell stopped. Everyone was quite silent; there was none of the usual gossip among lingering groups on the path through the churchyard. The only sounds came from the cuckoos and from Cotter showing somebody how to carry a banner. It was the first time I had seen a crowd of my fellow-countrymen since the blow fell. I looked round. Pink, stolid, rustic faces: had they any particular expression? If a visitor from another planet had been dropped suddenly in that churchyard, would he have guessed, by looking at them, that anything special was up? They weren't talking. But they never do talk much. I think they all did look rather puzzled. Decorous but puzzled.

We squeezed into the dim, stuffy, rustling church. It was packed already and there were many more to come, but the ubiquitous Cotter appeared, heading a procession of Scouts who carried extra chairs from the Parish Hall. He directed their disposition, up the aisle and under the tower. His expression said:

'I alone foresaw this and provided for it. Where would you all be without me?'

The Guides marched in and then came the British Legion. And I think a thrill of something a little like excitement did go through the church. There aren't many Legionaries in this tiny village. There seem to be more names on the War Memorial outside than there are men who came back. Most are fathers of families. Many have grown-up children. For twenty years they have been pursuing peaceful activities, shearing sheep and shoeing horses and building walls and selling onions. Some are growing fat and some are growing grey. But they were soldiers once, and now they are soldiers again, for if an invasion comes tomorrow they are all the troops we have.

They tramped and shuffled in rather shyly, and were pushed into the pews reserved for them by Cotter, and provided with hymn books by Cotter, who seemed to be so much in charge of proceedings that it was quite a surprise to see the Vicar appear and to realise that Cotter was not going to read the prayers and preach the sermon.

The Vicar was 'very upset', according to Nurse Ross, who heard it from a crony in the village. His young face was haggard and tense as he strode up the aisle. He knelt and we all knelt and prayed in silence while the cuckoos shouted and a dog barked in the sunny world outside. Then we all got up and sang: 'Through the Night of Doubt and Sorrow'.

We got down onto our knees again. The Vicar, low and hurriedly, read a number of special prayers. I could not hear them very distinctly, but they sounded as if they had been concocted by Cosmo Cantuar. I resorted to my own petitions which were incoherent and inconsistent. I prayed for a sudden Divine intervention – a new destruction of Sennacherib. I apologised for the childishness of such a prayer. I prayed to become a less despicable object. I again apologised for the childishness and egotism of supposing that it matters very much what kind of an object I am. And my thoughts strayed to Arnold Bennett. Because once, when I was fulminating against the iniquities of a mutual acquaintance, I said:

'I wonder the earth doesn't open and swallow X up.'

Whereat Arnold smiled. He jerked a thumb heavenward and said in his suave squeak:

'My dear Margaret! In the eyes of That-Fellow-Up-There, there is no more difference between you and X than there is between two fleas.'

A just rebuke. And I remember that he once told me that he liked to repeat to himself that verse from the Psalms: 'Be still and know that I am God.' I tried repeating it, but I don't think it did me much good. Perhaps it has a delayed action. And I went on thinking about dear Arnold and wondering what he would say to all this if he were here now. Why are all the best people dead and not here to share their courage and wisdom with us?

After the prayers four people advanced to the altar – two elderly Legionaries and two little Guides, each couple carrying a banner. They stood rigidly in a row with their backs to us while we sang that hymn which always means 'an occasion'.

We have been singing it all our lives, at Coronations, Jubilees, and school prize givings. It accompanies all our moments of communal emotion.

We sang it at the Memorial Service for T killed in Palestine in March, 1918. At that time there was no choir and the hymn sounded thin and shrill, for the congregation were mostly women. We sat, a bereaved black row, in the front pew and heard our friends quavering forlornly behind us about 'our hope for years to come'.

And eight months afterwards I heard it sung again. In the drizzle of that grey November morning I stood with Rhianon, my college roommate, in a little cluster of people outside St Aldgate's Post Office, in Oxford. We were waiting. The crowd kept growing. We had our flags all ready; we had bought them the night before – the flags of all the allies and a Welsh Lion for Rhianon. The Oxford clocks tolled out eleven. The Post-Office window was very dirty and a bodiless hand with a piece of wash leather suddenly came up from inside to clean it. There was a rumble of laughter from the crowd which stopped, like a sound-film cut off, when the hand reappeared and fixed up a notice scrawled in ink on half a sheet of notepaper. There was a second of absolute silence, then a surge forward, and a mutter, as those who could read passed the news back to the others, and the mutter swelled into a roar and the roar into a yell which seemed to go on all day without stopping. Windows flew up and heads came out and colour flowered all along the grey old street as the flags came tumbling over the window sills. And faintly, over that unending yell, came a vibration, as one by one the steeples and towers of Oxford woke up, Magdalen, St Mary's, Christchurch, broke into clamour and rocked under the November sky. And sometime on that day we were in St Mary's, which was packed from end to end with young recruits who were training in the empty colleges, boys who would not now have to go to the front and be killed as T had been killed. How they sang! How they shouted!

> Time, like an ever-rolling stream,
> Bears all its sons away.
> They fly forgotten ...

I cried on that day. But now I must not cry.

The Legionaries and the Guides advanced and laid their banners on the altar. The Vicar mounted the pulpit and began to speak to us, eagerly, humbly, and sincerely. It does not matter very much what he said. The tones of his voice said a great deal. He may have been upset but not from any selfish dismay. He felt that our souls were in his care and that it was his duty to comfort and sustain us. The responsibility appalled him, as well it might. But it did us good to see him tackle his job so courageously. Listening I thought that 'an honest man's the noblest work of God' and then wondered if it was Sidney H Smith who said: 'An honest God's the noblest work of man'.

Strange – the levity of the human mind. Strange that my attention should stray off to wisecracks, even to profound wisecracks, at a moment when I am more wretchedly unhappy than I ever was in my life before. T's death was nothing to this. Because we thought then that he had died to save Democracy.

※

The cuckoo was still hard at it when we got out of church and climbed the hill again. As it still wanted half an hour to tea we turned off at the stile by the Twelve Apostles to go for one of our little waddles. I asked David what he thought of the service.

'Oh ... heart-rending.'

5

Claire's father has come down. He thinks Surrey is no longer a safe place for the children. He says there will be constant dogfights over all the counties between London and the coast, and that planes driven off by the London defences will jettison their bombs all over here. And in case of invasion the wooded hills here would be important strategically. Parachutists might be dropped here to get behind our troops in the plains below, defending the coast. He says I would never dare to let the children out of my sight and this might well be declared a military zone. He wants me to get the children off, farther west, immediately. David agrees with him and we have decided on the little seaside town of Porthmerryn, where I lived some years when I was a girl and still have friends.

They want me to go with the children and to stay with them as long as there is any chance of an invasion. I don't like leaving David but I suppose they are right. The stories of lost children in Flanders are gruesome. I must stick to them like a burr.

✕

Charles is delighted at the idea of going to Porthmerryn. He loves to be on the move, and entertains a hope that there will be no kindergarten there. But the girls cried bitterly at the parting from their ponies and Geraldine the rabbit, and Rupert the (female) kitten. They begged to be allowed to take these last two with them, and at last I relented towards Rupert. But the portly Geraldine must be left here in the care of Cotter. I simply daren't saddle myself with a lot of livestock till I am sure that we shan't all be fleeing from German invaders.

I gave them a little lecture on the chins-up-we-are-all-in-the-front-line theme. Later on Lucy brought me a postcard which she had written to a school crony. It said:

The waw is getting very bad and we are lerning to nit.

If you think of it as the waw it does not seem so frightening somehow.

6

I have sent them all off with Miss Wright. I am staying here to pack and make various arrangements and shall go down to Porthmerryn next week. I can't count on being able to come back here easily, as we might be quite cut off if there was an invasion. So there is really a lot to do.

Cotter drove them to Woking where they were able to get an express. He reports that they had quite an eventful start to their journey. While they were waiting on the platform a train full of soldiers came in. The men were filthy and ragged and unshaven, many of them wounded and hastily bandaged up. They were shouting and cheering wildly, and all the people on the station platform were cheering and rushing forward with coffee and rolls and fruit and cigarettes. A huge, north-country giant jumped down onto the platform and kissed Lucy, pressing a Belgian franc into her hand.

'For thee, lass. Keep it. A soovenier from Dunkirk sitha.'

So *some* of our men are getting away! Cotter says that hundreds of trains are going through, all full of men back from Dunkirk. He says they were going through all night on our little branch line, a train every few minutes. He says a man in the village was down on the coast yesterday and he says they are arriving at all the towns along the sea, just tumbling in, brought by every sort of boat, fishing boats, pleasure steamers, even rowboats. And he says the Calais-Dover boats are being used: the old *Canterbury* came into

Brighton yesterday so packed she could hardly get along.

It is fantastic to think of the *Canterbury* in such a drama. She is the most comfortable of the Dover-Calais boats and people catching the Calais-Rome express always crossed in her. The very name conjures up memories of all the continental holidays we ever had. For we always felt our holiday had really begun when we found ourselves on the *Canterbury* and saw the white Dover cliffs growing smaller and knew that the English Channel was soon going to be put between us and work and duty and domesticity and the telephone.

I hope Lucy has taken care of her Belgian franc. It ought to be preserved as an heirloom in our family. I gather from Cotter that Ellen and Claire were a little piqued that Lucy should be singled out for such an honour. Why shouldn't they be kissed by strange soldiers? Poor dears! They won't know for a year or two yet. Claire is prettier than Lucy, Ellen is cleverer. They both have more amiable dispositions. But, 'If you have it, you don't need to have anything else; and if you don't have it, it doesn't much matter what else you have.' One of life's little practical jokes.

7

Streams of friends have come to see us today, and meeting them reminds me of the Munich Crisis in 1938. I keep remembering bits of it that I had forgotten. It was all so quick, such a nightmare, that one didn't get clear impressions. But now I recognise that look in friends' eyes, the mutual discovery that friendship can furnish no relief in universal misfortune. All the sources of relaxation, amusement, and stimulation are dried up and social intercourse is as flat as yesterday's soda water.

This is enhanced by the fact that we are all keeping a check on our emotions. We are a little guarded in what we say for fear of inadvertently annoying people, or straining nerves already taut, or deepening the general depression. We avoid controversy or provocative sallies; what would normally be stimulating arguments might easily sharpen into quarrels just now. One tries to short-circuit emotion rather than to share it. The 'genial current of the soul' is dammed up, and we fall back on bromides and bright little jokes.

I dare say when everything has got much worse we shall all be so busy giving one another practical help, sharing food and shelter and binding up each other's wounds, that we shan't miss the old peace-time pleasures of friendship so much.

There is another thing which I now remember from Munich. These sudden ordeals reveal people's characters like an X-ray photograph, so that one realises what they are made of. There are some who draw all their vitality from social contact, from sources outside themselves. They are charming and amusing and it is always a pleasure to meet them; they are appreciative too, and affectionate, so that one comes to regard them as having a tonic influence, because one feels so much at one's best in their company. But they are really like those road signs that are made of little plates of metal which light up and glow in the headlamps of an oncoming car but have no real light in themselves and go out after the car has gone. Such people have really very melancholy natures; they are not inwardly happy or satisfied or at peace, so they are driven outward to seek sustenance. And, since they need to be amused and liked, they take pains to be amusing and likeable. But in moments of universal disaster they seem to be completely extinguished. All the wit and gaiety and sympathy go out of them. They can find no escape from their own chronic inward melancholy. Whereas the people whose sources of life are within, in themselves, still shine out, a little dimmed, but steadily. They comfort you by being what they always were, anxious and sorrowful maybe, but still solidly there.

Such a one is Anna, who came down from town for the day. She is one of the best people I know: calm, poised, warm-hearted, clear-headed, and generous. She wasn't, naturally, as lively as usual today. But she was good fun in a quiet way. She reminded me about Pearl, a little servant, a regular alley-cat of a girl from a terribly poor slum home. When Pearl heard that Hitler said he would be in London by August 15, she said, in amusement rather than indignation:

'Eh! The cheeky monkey!'

This cheers us both up. We agreed that it is an example of the unsuggestibility which may be our great national safeguard. We may be able to stand the bombs if we don't get a superstitious fear of the men who drop them, or start thinking of Hitler as the invincible superman. We must remember that monkeys have always had this habit of getting up aloft and dropping things on the heads of their betters. I chalk Pearl up on the list with Cotter, Nurse Ross, and Miss Wright.

Our survival is in their hands.

8

Anna, being very much to the Left, sees this war as a sort of sideshow in the class war. But she is free from the irritating complacency of the Left Intellectuals, their aggressiveness, and their habit of imputing deliberate greed and self-interest to anyone who ventures to disagree with them. She is very gloomy about France. She says the class war there is impeding their efficiency. The Communists are sabotaging the war effort and the rich people would rather have Hitler than Socialism. She also retailed some hair-raising gossip which is going round London about traitors in France, both in the army and in politics. I simply can't believe it. I rather think she does, though.

Beryl, who lives six miles from here, came to tea. She is sustained, even now, by knowing more than anybody else. There are people who would be jaunty in hell, so long as they could run about spreading titbits of inside information about what Asmodeus said to Lucifer the other day. She too decries the French; she says their morale is bad and they run away from the German tanks. I cited a news bulletin which said that they had fought a brilliant action with tanks, just after the German break-through. She said yes – one. They have one very good general, who commanded this action, and is a tank expert. I think she said he is called Géle, if that is how it is spelt. He has been urging them for years to mechanise their army, but has been kept back because the older men are jealous of him. Now Reynaud has made him something or other, but it is too late, Beryl says.

Her sour wisecracks rattled like hailstones. She abused everything and everybody including 'the Americans in their bomb-proof pulpit.' 'They will not find it so bomb-proof,' she said, 'if Hitler gets all Europe.'

When at last she went to catch her bus home, we saw her go without regret. Her kind of rattling gossip used to be fun, in its way, but fun of that sort has gone pop.

Then, in the evening, Jacynth and Andrew walked over, bringing with them their pathetic Austrian refugee couple, so forlorn and neat, with polite little smiles and bows, and that bleak, bare look of people who have escaped in their best clothes and have no others, so have to keep very tidy. I can spot a refugee now at sight: the anxious eyes, the courteous smile, elegant town clothes in the country, and the extreme neatness of refined people who haven't a penny. They brightened up when they saw the maps of the Tyrol and the

Salzkammergut in our hall, and we talked about good walks and climbs and sleeping huts. Mr Refugee said gaily:

'I know that country like my pocket.'

Their position is ghastly. If Hitler gets here one cannot bear to think what their fate will be. And already they are suffering from the horrible stench of suspicion which is beginning to haunt all 'foreigners'. There are stories going about of refugees who have turned out not to be genuine at all, but Nazi agents. They are afraid that poor little Mr Refugee may have to be interned, for there is a frenzied round-up going on of all enemy aliens. But they face the prospect with a stoical dignity.

'It's for the safety of all,' said Mrs Refugee calmly. 'Ours as well as yours. All had better go, for there is no time to make distinctions. Later perhaps inquiries can be made and those who are genuine can be released. Anyway, we know that in this country he will not be cruelly treated.'

I do hope not. But the thing is being done at such panic speed that I fear there may be considerable hardship. Already he may not ride Andrew's bicycle into Guildford to do their shopping. No alien may 'own or control a bicycle'. He says he doesn't own it and can't control it, for it always runs away with him down the hills.

I walked round the garden with Jacynth. She is very gloomy, more gloomy than I am. No. She is only as gloomy as I am. But when other people are as gloomy as I am it seems worse, because in my own case I am able to temper it by thinking that I am a fool, and ignorant, and probably wrong.

She shattered me by endorsing the opinion of Anna and Beryl about France. She has a trustworthy friend who has just come back from Paris and gives a most alarming report. She says that France in 1940 is not the France of 1914, and is not going to put up anything like the same fight. They are thoroughly sick of war and have trusted so entirely to the Maginot Line that they can't face the idea of invasion; they are totally unprepared for it, mentally and physically. That is why they would not bother to make tanks. They thought they would not need them in defensive war, sitting behind their line; and they never had any intention of waging offensive war.

She says that a powerful party there has always been against the Anglo-French alliance and would rather play ball with Germany at our expense. They have never liked us much and think we have done far too little in the war so far. In fact, the German propaganda, England will fight to the last Frenchman, has taken root.

Her friend says that Paris is full of green-faced people saying: 'Trop tard. C'est fini. Nous sommes trahis.' And nobody tells them to 'go and say it in the toilet'. She says Hitler must surely know all this and will therefore certainly try to knock them out. If he can, then he may be hoping that he need not take the trouble to invade us and that we will make a deal with him at their expense.

All this is simply frightful and I do hope her informant is an alarmist. Still, if I am honest, I must admit to myself that I have been stifling qualms for months and years about the French. I never did like that Maginot Line. It was too like Hadrian's Wall and the decline of the Roman Empire. And it worried me that they would not pay their taxes. Even after the war started they wouldn't, when we were paying a minimum of seven shillings sixpence in the pound. If 'the test of democracy is public virtue', then it didn't seem to me that they were standing up to that test very well. But then they had a far heavier measure of conscription than we had. They stumped up their man power.

We always knew they didn't like us. No amount of soft soap in our press and theirs could disguise that fact. And many of our people couldn't get on with them. Very few of our men who fought in France in the last war have a good word to say for them. I'd rather have the Germans any day is a sentiment which I've heard again and again from old soldiers. They say that the French locked up their wells and charged a franc for a glass of water to the men who came to defend them. And we feel about their war debts to us as the Americans feel about our war debts to them. But the fact that our two peoples are not mutually sympathetic has never affected my belief that it is the joint duty of the two great democracies of Europe to try to keep things decent, or that Hitlerism is not as much a challenge to their way of life as it is to ours. As a friend's French maid put it, 'Bien sûr, on sait là-bas que l'un sans l'autre est foutu.'

What worried me most was the reputed corruption of their politicians and their cynicism about it. There is a point beyond which one cannot say: That is not our way of doing things but it may be all right. A friend of ours who lives in Paris told us that at the beginning of the war it was a current joke there to say of a prominent Minister: 'It's all right now because we pay him more than the Germans do.'

I could not think that funny. A nation which enjoys a joke like that can't be in very good case. It would be unthinkable, for instance, for us to make such a joke about Halifax, or the Americans about Cordell Hull.

Many of us are uneasy about France, yet the propagandists have been serving out the most fervid ballyhoo about how close England and France are drawing together, how we are bound in a union which will surprise the world. Somerset Maugham's sentimental little book, *France at War*, is typical of the stuff they have been feeding us. But what else could they do? Tell the truth? I suppose they had to keep up this humbug. But it can we afford humbug in this war?

'Well,' I said to Jacynth, 'even if Hitler does knock France out, we couldn't make a deal with him, could we?'

She said: 'It would be deserting our allies. We've got to go on fighting as long as we have anything to fight with.'

'Besides,' I said, 'it would only be another Munich. He would never stick to any agreement. Our Empire would fall to pieces and we should never get it together for another war effort. The Dominions and the Americans would wash their hands of us. Hitler would gobble us up whenever it suited him and we shouldn't have a friend in the world to drop a tear on our dishonoured graves.'

'I'm afraid, though,' she said, 'we may have to fight alone.'

'Should we have a chance of winning, if France goes out?'

'I don't know. We'll have none if we don't fight.'

'It may be a grave, either way, but if we fight there will be some tears on it?'

Jacynth looked as if she thought all this about tears and graves was a bit fanciful. She said:

'We shan't all be dead, I suppose, even if Hitler wins.'

I went from bad to worse and said that subjection to Hitler would be 'the Nightmare Life-in-Death that thicks man's blood with cold'.

She said firmly that she didn't know about all that but that we simply cannot desert Poland and Norway and Holland and Belgium.

Andrew and David brought out some sherry and we drank it on the terrace. I reminded them if of the song in the comic opera, *Polly*, when a dispirited army is told that it is entirely cut off and must conquer or die and is instructed to sing a rousing battle song. So it shuffles round the stage wailing out a perfunctory Cockney chorus:

Nao rertreat! Nao rertreat!
We must conquer er die fer there's nao rertreat.

We all began to chant it, shuffling round the terrace with our sherry glasses.

Mr and Mrs Refugee suddenly appeared. They had been for a little walk to look at the swimming pool. We stopped shuffling and felt uncommonly foolish. It was impossible to explain why we were prancing round and singing that doggerel. Being 'foreigners' they recovered poise first and ignored the incident. They asked us to solve for them a problem. In England is a duke's son always an earl?

9

The house is like a grave without the children. I wander from room to room packing and sorting. It will be horrible for poor David when we have all gone. He won't come here any more but will live in London near his work, and his mother wants to go to London, too.

Cotter gloomily helps me to nail down packing cases. He is very much depressed, for he loved riding with the children and says it was the pleasantest part of the war, as if the war had abounded in a choice of pleasant aspects. He says that Lucy was shaping to be a proper little horsewoman, which is scarcely fair to Claire who, taught by her Australian father, is much the best rider of the three. But Cotter picks Lucy for the same reason that the soldier from Dunkirk did.

Also he disapproves of our departure. He says there is no need for it. What if an invasion is attempted? Didn't I see the Legion in church?

'Has the Legion got any guns yet?' I ask.

'Well,' says Cotter, scratching his head, 'just at the moment, Madam, that's a bit awkward. But we'll have plenty before Jerry gets here.'

'How many have you got now?'

'Why ... we've got George Pike's rook rifle and ... and ... yes ... George Pike's rook rifle we've got.'

'Then if a parachutist came down ...'

'We'd shoot him with George Pike's rook rifle.'

'And if ten parachutists ... a hundred parachutists ...'

'Excuse me, Madam. That couldn't happen.'

He explains that only one parachutist can possibly come at a time. An aeroplane which carried more than one would fly so slowly that Our Boys would get it before it crossed the coast. He is talking through his hat, of course, but he is so sure of himself that he has a slightly sedative effect upon me.

He has found out who it is that puts the Nazi propaganda in the Legion's letter-box. It is a woman living in the village. He has reported it to the police and is now very indignant and says they are slack because they don't arrest her. I expect he gave them a lot of advice and got slightly snubbed. David says he doesn't suppose she has done anything for which she could be arrested. There is apparently no law against putting subversive literature into people's letter-boxes at midnight. It does not prove that she is a spy or a traitor. She is doubtless being watched, and if she does anything she shouldn't she will be pulled in.

I know her well by sight. She strides about the lanes and woods, always alone, eyeing everyone she meets with a startlingly malevolent expression. She looks half crazy: tall, handsome, untidy, expensively dressed, aged, I should think, about fifty.

We encountered her first when the children and I were primrosing in the woods. She appeared suddenly on the woodland path and cast at us such a look of extreme hatred and spite that I nearly spat after her through my fingers, as a protection against the Evil Eye.

Claire said:

'Why did that woman glare at us so? Is she a witch?'

Which echoed my thought. And afterwards, when I saw her again, always glaring, I came to the conclusion that in the Middle Ages she would have been a witch. A woman with a grudge against all the world.

⁂

I have been pondering a lot about the right thing to do if there is an invasion. Even at Porthmerryn there might be trouble. Obviously the one thing not to do is to be a refugee crowding out onto the roads and being run over by tanks and arriving at towns where there is no food and being bombed there. It would be best to stay put even if the Germans came, and hide food. But we might be ordered suddenly to evacuate, and so we ought to prepare to be as mobile as possible and to be able to live on our own humps and not be a burden and a problem to other people. I have made out a list of things we ought to do.

1. Money. Have quite a large sum, in notes, safely locked up in the house, ready to be sewed into my stays.
2. See that each member of the household has a pair of good strong shoes or boots which will stand up to long and hard wear.
3. Have a rucksack or knapsack ready for everyone, even Charles, so that we can carry our own things. Have in each rucksack a list of the things that person has to pack in it – a change of linen, waterproof, warm woolly spare socks, comb, soap, toothbrush, and torch. In my own sack I must have sewing materials, some simple medicines, sticking plaster, brandy, etc.
4. Think out iron ration of compressed food we can carry and have it ready.
5. Remember gas masks, ration books, and identification cards.

Then we can go anywhere at any time, across country if roads are impossible, and will be tolerably self-sufficient. I am sure that if every household would do this it would be a wise precaution.

We are all enormously relieved at what seems to be happening at Dunkirk. It is a miracle. If we can do this, maybe we can rise to a few more miracles. And we have an army again. When it is all sorted out and re-equipped it will be a pretty tough army.

This is the third time David and I are parted, not knowing when we are going to meet again, not knowing what dangers he is going to face in London, only knowing that we each have to plough a long, bitter furrow alone, when we have grown so used to double harness that we don't know how to set about it. The first time was in the Munich Crisis in 1938. The second time was when war broke out in 1939. But this is the worst time, because he will worry about us so, with this invasion scare.

10

I went into Guildford to get one hundred pounds in bank notes for my emergency invasion pocket. The road there is transformed. There are barriers at intervals all the way; some are only pine logs and brushwood, but they are being rapidly replaced by concrete. All signposts have been removed. Little forts and blockhouses are going up everywhere. Obstructions have been put in the larger fields. We have evidently learnt something from the campaign in the Low Countries. I would not have thought so much could be done in a week.

Everyone in Guildford was reading a special early edition of an evening paper. There has been a raid on some village in Kent and children have been killed. The first children, I think, on this island. I went into Woolworth's and the girl who served me, seeing my paper, asked:

'What's 'e bin doing now?'

We talk about 'him' too much. In the last war we talked about 'them'. He is getting too much of a hold on our imaginations. We ought to take a leaf out of Pearl's book and think of him as a cheeky monkey. But he is a spellbinder, an illusionist; he does things which we know are phony and yet we can't show him up. His pact with Stalin is phony. The Axis is phony. The Italians loathe the Germans. But both Stalin and Mussolini continue obligingly to play his game. His Third Reich is the phoniest thing of all. His fellow thugs, Goering, Ribbentrop, and all, are known to have arranged their getaway, and have huge fortunes safely stowed in neutral countries to which they can scuttle when the crash comes. His finances beat the Indian rope trick. His house is built of cards, but he huffs and he puffs and he blows the world down. How does he do it? Perhaps so much of Europe was phony anyway that it would have gone down at the first determined huff and puff, by whomsoever delivered.

Well, Napoleon walked through Europe as if it were butter until he came up against something that wasn't butter.

I gave the girl the paper and the other girls came up to read it too, fair heads and dark heads, all beautifully permed, clustered together, reading about our Holy Innocents.

'Fancy!' said a fat girl with freckles. 'Whatever were the wardens doing, I wonder.'

I made the mistake of setting her down for a fool.

A pretty, rather shrewish brunette said sharply:

'Sil-lee! The wardens can't stop the bombs dropping.'

'Ow!' said the fat girl. 'I thought they was supposed to catch 'em and chuck 'em back.'

A titter went round the group. The brunette flounced away.

I concluded that she was a warden, or perhaps it is her boy who is a warden, and the others have heard rather too much about it. Anyway, Fatty is not such a fool as she looks. British thick-headedness … you never know.

Three gypsy women got into the bus coming it back. They were the first thoroughly cheerful people I have seen for a long time. Their bright sharp eyes glanced about everywhere. Bright and sharp but not quite human. They talked a debased tinker's lingo, not the 'deep Romany' that the Welsh gypsies talk. I noticed they called London 'The Smoke' as the Liverpool gypsies do. And I caught several words of obvious Latin origin. They called a penny a deener (*denarius*) and one of them said she must get off the bus at the eggels, which turned out to be a church (*ecclesia*). I wonder if these are relics of some *lingua franca* that was once talked by all the rogues and vagabonds of Europe, just as Latin was talked by all the scholars.

One was feeding her baby, aged about six months, with bits of rich plum cake which she had previously chewed up herself. You couldn't ask to see a finer baby. She reminded me of the lovely gypsy girl I saw in the inn yard of Chipping Camden in the Cotswolds. I leaned out of a window and watched her alternately suckling her baby and feeding it beer out of a mug. The inn chambermaid, who was leaning out beside me, commented approvingly:

'Ar! That child is being brought up as Nature intended.'

✕

At the bus stop I realized that I should get home too late to hear the news bulletin, so I went into the local pub to hear the wireless in the bar, and ordered a gin and ginger beer. Several local worthies and two hikers were there. Suddenly the door was pushed open and in strode – the Witch! A hush went over the company and everybody eyed her. I'm sure they all know about the Legion letter-box. She ordered a gin and Italian and stood by the bar drinking it and tapping her foot impatiently on the ground, returning our dirty looks with interest. There is a horse pond just up the road, where I dare say they used to duck witches two hundred years ago. All her movements are harsh, clumsy, and uncoordinated, and I think her eyes are not quite focused.

The hikers seemed to be aware of some kind of tension in the air and one of them turned on the wireless, though it was not quite news time. We crashed into part of an entertainment programme for the Forces. A comedian was gabbling in that desperate, 100 mph keep-it-*up*-keep-it-*up* way they have:

'I meantersay if a *hospital nurse* married a baker their child would be a bread POULTICE.'

Ha! Ha!

11

Oh, but I am frightened, though. I am simply terrified. I suppose everyone is really quite as frightened as I am, but as we never talk about it I don't know. Hitler is no fool. He must know that we won't make a deal with him even if he does knock France out. So I'm sure he will try invasion here at once, before we have time to rearm our men from Dunkirk, before we have time to put concrete instead of pine logs across the roads, before the Witch is locked up. He will never have a better chance. We are in for an unspeakably horrible experience.

Well? The French are facing it. The Poles have been through it. Why shouldn't we?

But I have *children*.

So have Polish mothers got children. In Poland they are shooting men like David by the thousand. They are carrying off little girls hardly older than Ellen and Claire to German brothels. They will do the same here, and worse, if they get the chance.

My mother's grave is in the cemetery here. She and Father took a house in these parts in 1928, and she died suddenly just after they moved in. I went up to the cemetery today. It is a lonely place away among the pine woods. One half of it, where there are no graves, is still heather and bracken. Nobody was about, so I had a good long cry, lying on the grass beside the grave.

I told her what is happening to her child and to the grandchildren she so longed for. I kept sobbing:

'O Mother, Mother! Where are you? Can't you help us?'

It is infantile to cry for one's mother, but I suppose that most people do it at least once in their adult lives. Nothing can erase our earliest impressions. The conviction persists that she could have set all right, that she would have been an unshakable rock, calm, unafraid, never letting danger come near her children. My reason tells me that if she were here now she would be just as shattered as the rest of us. She was a fine, brave creature, but she was only a woman, not a protecting goddess.

I can't even picture her very clearly now. Mostly I remember her as the fair, mild, blue-eyed woman she was in her middle age. The later memories are sad; in the last years she was a tiny old woman, wasted with disease and always, always silently grieving for T. But sometimes a very early scene flashes upon me, when we children were quite little and she was younger than I am now, and she used to run about, her eyes sparkling, just as Lucy runs about today.

Now she is gone. I don't know where.

Can the dead help us? When good and brave people die, do all their virtue and courage stop? I can't believe it. Not only does their memory, all that they were, live on in our minds, but maybe all that they still are is also available to us. And to brave men it is given to draw upon those reserves of strength and force which are the common possession of the living and the dead.

Catholics believe that the Church Triumphant stands behind the Church Militant. If we use all the courage we have, even if we know that it is not nearly sufficient for the test before it, perhaps we shall find that more is given to us from elsewhere. But we must first use what we have, like the servants in the parable. We must have faith. Unless men have faith that strength will be given, they cannot use even the poor strength they have.

These thoughts presented themselves to me as I lay on the grass by her grave. It is strange how thoughts come, blowing into our minds from ... *what other mind*?

On her gravestone we have written:

I will lift up mine eyes unto the hills, from whence cometh my help. My help cometh from the Lord, which made heaven and earth. The Lord shall preserve thee from all evil: he shall preserve thy soul.

And on T's grave, far away in Palestine, is written:

The reward of fortitude is immortality for it is admired of gods and of men.

We must just creep on from day to day, doing faithfully that day's task, using to the utmost what strength and courage we have, and hope to get more from the Lord when our own runs out.

I kissed the cold stone and went back to my packing.

12

We all find it difficult to sleep, these days. I expect we shall learn how to, in time, when we have got used to living through history. Some people take sedatives and some do not. There are two schools of thought about it. The opposition says that this state of things will go on for a long time, at best, and that we had better learn right now to sail under our own steam. Also the stock of bromides in the country might give out, so we must avoid becoming too dependent on them. But others say that we are all suffering at the moment from a severe shock, and that it need not last, though strain and anxiety and danger will. Their argument is that to secure a few good nights of sound sleep now, before the curtain goes up, will steady our nerves.

David points out that there were no bromides in 1588. But I say that's all very well, they drank like fishes for one thing, and for another they were tougher than we are in every way, tougher than we ever want to be. School children used to get a half holiday to see a hanging. Public executions were attended like football matches. People were even publicly burned to death. And the sight of a neighbour in the pillory with his ears cut off was a commonplace. Besides which, they all had the comfortable belief that their enemies would ultimately go to hell and be tormented for ever.

Much more is being required of us than ever was required of our forefathers. We are facing a danger which is quite as horrible as anything they ever had to face. If the Spaniards had conquered us in 1588 they could not have done more awful things than the Germans will do if they get here, and the Elizabethans did not have to stand up to bombing and poison gas. Yet we have somehow managed to become much more humane and tolerant and civilised than our ancestors were. I think we have every right to call in the help of science, so long as we keep a sense of proportion about it.

I have not asked the doctor for a bromide yet, but I shall if I don't sleep better after I get down to Porthmerryn, for

I haven't been able to get more than a cat nap for a week. Conscientiously I do the relaxing drill they advise you to do. I grow drowsy. But then I start awake with a convulsive jerk.

Last night I got so desperate that I went out onto the roof of the music room. I thought if I couldn't sleep I might at least get some air, for the blackout makes our bedrooms stuffy. There is a ladder up to the roof and a sort of penthouse with a rattan sofa. I took up a quilt and a pillow and dragged the sofa out under the sky and watched 'the moon set and the Pleiades'.

One by one the stars vanished and the night ticked on from moment to moment till it came to that mysterious pause it makes just before the start of a new day, as if the earth hesitated for a few seconds, and then got the order to roll on. Then a cock crew down in the valley and I heard the ponies snorting in their stable. The light came back into the bowl of the air, drop by drop, till I could see the black ridges of the pine woods on the hills. A wind came and rustled the trees. The dawn smells of earth and moss and leaves began to rise up, and the morning star appeared in a sky of palest aquamarine. The world was rushing over to the sun and the upshot beam mounted higher and higher until all the little clouds in the zenith flushed pink.

Suddenly the air was full of sound: a deep vibrating hum, coming from the south. Across the pine ridges came about thirty of our bombers, under the fiery sky, flying in perfect formation, with the precision of a figure in a ballet. They were returning to their base from the battlefield. They swept on their way with an extraordinary effect of august power and calm and confidence.

Those men up there are happy. Even in the middle of all this they are happy. They have been risking their lives all night, but they are happy because they can use their manhood, their skill and daring and energy, and they are proud of their machines and proud of the men who made them.

I must not think only of suffering and wrecked homes and the anguish of women and children. I must not forget that men can be sublime. War is wicked and evil, and the world will be a better place when we have abolished war. But it has come upon us now and we can, if we will, meet it sublimely. *The reward of fortitude is immortality.* While we have men like these there will be glory. Oh yes, there will be glory, even if Hitler wins. They are deathless, these men, and they will make poetry for men in other ages. For victory and defeat are only names; they mean something which lasts for a day and then is forgotten. But the story of Leonidas at the Pass at Thermopylæ means the same thing now that it did more than two thousand years ago.

✠

I slept for a while and when I awoke it was broad sunshine. The parlour-maid was standing beside me disapprovingly with my early morning tea. She had not found me where a lady ought to be, in my bed, so she had plodded round with the tea tray looking for me. She must have had a job to haul it up the ladder. I suppose if she hadn't found me on the roof she would have hunted in the coal cellar and the stable and the pigsties.

Down at Porthmerryn we won't have any maids. We will get a little cottage and old Nanny and I will do the work. And after the war we shall be much too poor to have any maids. Hurrah! They've been the bane of my life, ever since I married. They disapprove of everything I do and give me notice because they have seen me strolling down Oxford Street licking a penny ice cone, which no 'gentry' would do. Why mustn't I walk down Oxford Street licking an ice?

After the war we shall be terribly poor, but there won't be any more gentry, and I shall be able to walk down Oxford Street licking anything I like.

If Oxford Street is still there – after the war.

13

The parting is over. Cotter drove us to Woking where David caught a train to London and I caught the express.

David's train went first. We said good-bye hastily. We have not talked very much these last days. There is nothing to say. The best comfort we can give each other is to ask for none. David made a grimace, as if the whole world was a bad smell, jumped into his train and said through the window:

'Kiss them for me.'

And his train went.

Now I am sitting in the waiting room. I have an actual, physical pain in my chest as if my heart had been torn out of my body. I wonder if it would hurt as much if it had been the children I was leaving. I wonder just how many millions of women in the world have this pain now because war has parted them from their husbands. But David is right. The mother of a child as young as Charles should stay with him as long as there is any chance of invasion.

✕

While I was waiting for my train at Woking a Dunkirk train came through. Those men the children saw must have been among the earliest to escape. I am glad they did not see these, who have been longest in that hell. There was no cheering this time. They were utterly exhausted, and stared out of the windows with blank, indifferent eyes. Most of them were French. Women took them coffee and cigarettes and they handed out postcards, hastily scribbled to their families in France, to say they are safe. Unsmiling, they muttered *Merci, Madame*, and sank back into their seats.

The train moved on. There was a fat, pasty-faced young man in a beret leaning out of the last window. As he caught my eye he turned thumbs up languidly. The gesture meant nothing except perhaps a parody of defiance. His expression was ironical ... hopeless. It haunts me still.

I asked the porter if all these troop trains had meant a great deal of dislocation on the line. He said rather loftily that it was nothing to Ascot Week.

I sat waiting on a bench with a lot of women who presented an utterly stolid face to the world. I wonder how stolid they were feeling inside. The two next to me were talking about her, not him, which is a good sign.

'... I said to her, I said, it's a good thing, I said, that I can see the funny side of it. Some wouldn't, I said. Fridays is the day Mrs Barclay works for me, I said, and always has done for a donkey's years before she ever worked for you, I said to her. But she ...'

The train came in. It was crammed with soldiers. I found a seat at last in a first-class carriage with six Tommies and an antediluvian person who protested at their presence and told them they ought to go third. They said all the thirds were full. Then they ought to go and stand in the corridor, said this survival of the Stone Age.

'I've been fighting,' said one, quite good-humouredly, 'and I'm going to give my bum a treat while I can.'

'The first class is reserved for officers,' complained the survival.

The soldiers laughed.

He appealed to me.

I laughed.

The ticket inspector came in and a complaint was lodged.

The inspector laughed.

When 'revolution' takes place in England this is all you see of it. Something new has become a joke. And people who imagine that the old order can't pass away without guillotines and barricades and citizens and comrades and liquidations, just can't realise that anything has happened, and go on earnestly flogging dead horses. My Communist acquaintances, who greatly dislike levity, would condemn all this laughter. They would complain that these soldiers are not class conscious. Quite true. They aren't. They are miles past that stage. We don't have to go toiling painfully back to 1917 to get rid of the Old School Tie.

Chapter Three

June: 'This Is Only the Beginning'

1

Porthmerryn faces the sea; it is a little fishing port in a coastline of granite cliffs. Its population is divided into three communities, Downalong, Upalong, and The Artists.

Downalong lives in the old town by the harbour. The houses tumble higgledy-piggledy down the side of the cliff like a box of bricks upset on a staircase. They are built of solid warm grey stone; the ground floors are fish cellars and a massive staircase often leads from the street to the house door and the living quarters on the first floor. These outside staircases give a peculiar and charming character to the streets which are narrow and crooked and very often not streets at all, but long irregular flights of steps.

There is a prevailing smell of fish and tar, and the scream of hundreds and hundreds of gulls is mingled with the noise of carts rumbling over the cobbles from the quayside to the railway station. The little boats lie on the wet sand inside the harbour at low tide. They put out into the bay at evening, and bring back their catch at dawn. By day the packing and carting go on.

On either side of the harbour there are sandy beaches where the summer visitors bathe from tents. Between these two bays runs out a rocky headland called 'the Island', where the huge fish nets are laid out on the short turf to dry. For net-making competes with fishing as a staple industry of the town. It is carried on in sheds close to the Island, and the people often sing as they work, so that the Island is haunted by the cry of gulls, screaming over the thunder of the surf on the beaches, and the chant of hymns in strong voices:

> Hide me, O my Saviour, hide,
> Till the storm of life is past.
> Safe into the haven guide. . . .

Or sometimes it is a more modern ditty:

> When my mother-in-law was ill,
> I pulled her through.
> Though I have no doctor's skill,
> I pulled her through.
> They sent for me at half-past four.
> When I got there my mother-in-law
> Was simply lying at death's door.
> I pulled her through.

And sometimes it is a very old one. *John the Beau* is a great favourite. The tune is called *The Helston Furry*; in the spring all the people dance to it in the streets of Helston church town, and a Furry means Flora, and it is the relic of an old, old Spring Festival.

> John the Beau went out one day;
> And he met with Sally Dover.
> He kissed her once, he kissed her twice,
> He kissed her three times over.

On fine days there is always a row of women who hang their great webs from hooks on the Customs House wall, down on the harbour. As they work they keep up a constant cross-fire of gossip and laughter with their cronies flinging fish from creels into butties, and the carters, and the old salts who stump up and down the quay outside the Sloop Inn. They speak in a sharp, high singsong and their idiom is picturesque.

'If you'd struck a knife into me in that hour, you'd have drawn no blood,' says a Downalong woman, if she wants to tell you that she has been surprised.

And I have heard a woman, leaning from a window, mocking some men below because they said the weather was too dirty to take the boats out:

'Ho! You put caendle in winder! If her go out you say dirty weather. If her don't go out you say you got no wind, hey?'

The last sentence runs up the scale, crescendo, to 'wind', and drops an octave to 'hey'.

I never knew a place more vividly alive than Downalong. There is always stir and drama and excitement among these swarthy Celtic people. At funerals it is considered correct for the chief mourners to fling themselves frequently down in the road on the way to the cemetery. Sympathizers walk on either side of them to raise them up after each paroxysm, dust them, and praise them for their grief.

They don't dislike the English but they call them foreigners and they deeply resent any foreign interference in their local affairs. Nobody knows beforehand how they are going to vote in an election. They go to the polling booths impartially wearing the colours of all the Candidates. But they vote solid, for their motto is One and All. And, as the fishing vote is decisive in this constituency, no candidate knows what his chances are likely to be.

They are deeply religious, and while generally on the side of anybody who is in trouble with the police, they are quite capable of breaking the windows of anybody who has offended against their moral code. Cruelty to children rouses them almost to lynching point. No child need ever go hungry in Porthmerryn. If times are hard in one home, all neighbouring doors are open at dinnertime.

✕

Upalong lies on the surrounding hills, and figures as the genteel part of the town. It consists of brick terraces, lodging houses, hotels, villas, bungalows, and a few solid stone mansions with large gardens. Here live some of the wealthier townspeople – lawyers, bankers, and doctors. But the standard resident of Upalong is the retired man who has come to Porthmerryn because living there is cheap and the golf links good. These ex-soldiers, sailors, schoolmasters, or Indian civil servants, with their wives and daughters, form a fluctuating colony with golf and bridge as principal diversions. They live among chintzes, knick-knacks, brass elephants, and ancient photographs in silver frames of relatives in Presentation gowns, until summer comes, when they rent their houses and vanish for three months. It is not at all the thing to be seen on either of the beaches in August.

The Artists live an uncertain life suspended between these two communities. They are no good to the Upalong girls, for they are either married or penniless. Often both. They live in Downalong because it is cheaper, drink at the Sloop Inn, and have an Arts Club in a fish loft.

They discovered Porthmerryn about the year 1890, and since then they have painted its gulls, boats, jetty, and steep streets for many Academies. Summer visitors sometimes buy their pictures, along with tins of cream, fragments of rock crystal, moss-agate brooches, and ships in bottles, manufactured in the Midlands.

2

Now I seem to have travelled fifteen years backward in time, because Porthmerryn has not changed one little bit. The rash of new bungalows has spread farther over the hills and along the cliffs. There is a new parking place and a new cinema and a better bus service to Penmorvah. But that is all. Downalong, Upalong, and The Artists are still here, going strong, as vital, as quiescent, as out at elbows as ever.

The war, the real war which began this spring, has not got here yet. It too must be travelling westward, but I have got here well ahead of it. Nobody is worrying. The shops are full of clotted cream and the streets are full of char-a-bancs and holiday makers in beach slacks. When I look at all these brown, tranquil faces I realise how strained and white everyone is looking up London way, how tense even the women at Woking Station.

There are, it's true, no fishing boats in the harbour. It seems they all went round to help in the Dunkirk evacuation and have not got back yet. But this is not the fishing season, and there is such a boom in the net industry that everyone is hard at work. The nets are used for camouflage; the pay is good and everyone is making pots of money. Even Upalong has taken to net making. A web hangs up in nearly every drawing room, among the silver photograph frames, and is proudly displayed as:

'My war work. But I give the money to the Red Cross, of course.'

On top of that there is a boom in summer visitors. Many habitués of the East Coast have come west this year. All the hotels and lodgings are full, and the curio shops are doing a roaring trade. In fact Porthmerryn thinks this is quite a good war. The blackout is only observed very sketchily. At night all Downalong is a blaze of light. A notice outside the Post-Office about parachutists looks like some kind of practical joke.

I feel like a ghost. Old friends greet me kindly and then ask in dismay if I have been ill. I'm looking so pale and thin they say. I don't think I look paler or thinner than anybody else east of Plymouth. People here seem rather fat and red.

Today I met Martha from Downalong, who used to be our maid in the old days. She asked what people in London think of the war.

'They're rather gloomy,' I told her.

'Gloomy? Why? They don't think Hitler is going to win, do they? We don't think so Downalong, not for a single minute.'

'I'm afraid there will be some pretty bad bombing.'

'Oh, Our Boys will soon stop that.'

Mrs Aitken, the *doyenne* of Upalong, said:

'The news lately has been rather *queer*, hasn't it? I was quite worried till Ronnie [her grandson] got out of Dunkirk.'

✖

Only two people have that look of shock and dismay which I have come to know so well. They are Mary and Magnus Keith, the oldest and dearest of all my Porthmerryn friends. Thank God, neither of their sons is in immediate danger: one is in the Far East and the other in one of our consulates in Greece. But Mary and Magnus have lived in many parts of Europe and understand what is happening only too well.

Magnus is sustained by a strange admiration for Mussolini. He was in Florence at the time of the Fascist march on Rome and saw Fascism as an admirable, energetic kind of Puritanism, an awakening of young people to ideals of service and sacrifice. For a long time he would not believe in the stories of floggings and dosings of castor oil, and the growth of corruption and oppression. Abyssinia shook him a bit, and the invasion of Albania really shocked him, but he still will not believe that Italy will ever fight for Hitler.

Everybody else wonders why Mussolini has not leaped to the aid of the victor already. But I suppose it is one thing for a dictator to bring his people into a war and another to make them fight. If he does come in nobody expects him to fight very hard.

Mary says little. She has aged since last I saw her and her hair is quite white, but her beautiful blue eyes have that same clear, innocent wisdom, and she occupies herself, as always, in helping other people. She has found me a little house, right in the fields at the very top of Upalong. It is so small that there is no room for me as long as Miss Wright is with us. But my friend Helga, who has a cottage just across the road, has offered me a bed till the summer holidays.

✖

So here we are, waiting for something to happen. Hitler may attack on the Somme, or he may invade us, or he may do both. Paris has been bombed. Details of the damage are scanty and obscure but we get the impression that it must have been pretty bad.

We got a sentimental sort of account of it from one of our ministers who was over there and was kept waiting for his lunch. He said that Paris had never looked lovelier and the people were quite unperturbed. But we don't get the sort of details which are reassuring. I have a horrible feeling that things are going very wrong. I believe Winston and all of our people are getting one frightful shock after another and don't know how much to warn us about it.

3

We are quite settled in our little house, and our life now runs in an orderly routine. I am roused every morning at 6.45 by Helga's wireless broadcasting in Norwegian. I begin to dress and when I hear Big Ben at 7am I fling on a dressing gown and rush down to hear the English news and find out if 'it' has happened in the night. Everybody seems to assume that the invasion will begin at dawn some day. Helga has been up and dressed for some hours and is already working at her net. Her cat sits opposite her, surveying the world with an unblinking, malevolent stare.

Hitler did not come in the night. So that means we have another day in which to prepare. A few more soldiers will have guns, a few more concrete barriers will go up. Helga is a linguist but I wonder if she understands Norwegian as well as she believes she does. She astounds me with items from the broadcast. I gather that Russia has declared war on New Zealand, and President Roosevelt has joined the RAF, and Goering has the mumps.

I finish dressing and do my room and go across to our house for breakfast. In the morning Miss Wright and the girls do lessons, Nanny takes Charles to the little school we have found for him (poor Charles!) and does the marketing, and I do up the work. To save the bother of cooking and washing we take our midday meal at a nice small hotel close to the beach. We take tea down with us and spend the afternoon on the beach, where we have a tent. After tea the girls go up for more lessons. If we are here next term I mean to send them to one of the many schools which have evacuated themselves here, and Miss Wright is trying to teach them to spell, for fear they should be flung out as mentally deficient. They do nothing but spelling, poor girls, morning, noon, and night. We have supper at seven and after we have washed up I go down to the Keiths' to hear the evening news.

The days tick by like the days a man spends in prison waiting for his trial. It is glorious weather and I should enjoy the bathing every afternoon if I could enjoy anything.

I go to bed early because Helga likes to lock up at ten o'clock. But I lie in bed reading till all hours. I have just finished *Persuasion*. Now I have started on *War and Peace*. It's queer to think of the novelists and poets and playwrights who will write about all this in the future, just as Tolstoi wrote of the Moscow Campaign. But there will be no Tolstois if Hitler wins; not for many a long day. Not in Europe. There might be in America, if the Yanks manage to hold out. And they will have to carry on all the art and culture and thought, and live on their own humps, mentally, for there won't be any more exchange of ideas across the Atlantic – that stimulating battledore and shuttlecock of thought and inspiration between the Old World and the New that there has been.

Still, if the treasures of the mind have got to be confided to the guardianship of one nation, the Yanks are probably as well fitted for the job as any people, because they spring from such a variety of races and have so much elbow room. Culture, in their hands, won't become poky or provincial; it will have a whole continent to spread itself in.

4

Hitler has attacked on the Somme. Now we shall know whether Anna and Beryl and Jacynth were well informed.

The Keiths, who have lived much in France, don't dismiss the idea of a French collapse as at all impossible. They say it is quite true that many of the French people dislike us intensely. Magnus said that when they were last there somebody had chalked 'À bas les Anglais' on a tarred fence outside their hotel. After it had been there about two months he got rather annoyed about it, so one day he chalked underneath it 'Vive les Boches.' Next morning both inscriptions had been rubbed out.

He dislikes the French. He says that vanity and avarice are their leading traits. He gets impatient with Mary and me for our pro-Gallicism and calls it purely sentimental. We talk about the invaluable part France has played in Western civilisation, and he says what is it? What unique contribution has she made to the world? We have better poets, Germany has better musicians, Italy has better painters, America has a better democracy and, he says, better cooking. All four nations can hold their own with her in science and philosophy.

I say it is humanism – and I gave them an illustration of what I mean. A cousin of mine went some years ago to visit a clinic in Paris for the treatment of delinquent children. At first she was somewhat shocked by the general appearance of inefficiency – the dirt and disorder, the equipment so cheap and shabby, the assistants slovenly in their manner, no white starch, white tiles, casebooks, or filing cabinets. But when she got into the inner sanctuary and saw the Great Man actually at work she was consumed with admiration. She said she had seen nothing like it anywhere in Europe. To watch him with the children and their poor mothers was like entering a new world. He was never condescending, but was profoundly humane without being in the least sentimental. He talked to them clearly and simply, using words which they could understand, and was so absolutely unafraid of truth that he was free from all roughness and nervousness in his approach to it.

It was quite a new thing to her to see a great intellect functioning in such a manner. Over here men who possess exceptional intellectual powers seem often to be embarrassed by them, to carry them clumsily, almost as if they were a deformity. Thus a superior intellect actually tends sometimes to cut a man off from his fellow-men. It makes him shy and pedantic, so that he finds it difficult to communicate his ideas to simple people.

This may be a characteristic which we inherit from our German ancestors, for intellectual snobbery is, I think, a peculiarly Teutonic fault. The Germans don't think a man can have a great brain unless he is quite incomprehensible to all but a chosen few. The more obscure he is, the more they idolize him.

But we are pretty bad about this, and our medical men are among the worst sinners. They have no notion of sharing truth with the world. Nurse Ross once told me of a great Edinburgh surgeon who, after performing an operation on a young man, gave a highly technical and incomprehensible account of it to the patient's parents, a humble, bewildered old couple. They listened very carefully and thanked him, but at the doorway the poor old woman turned and said:

'Eh, doctor, ye suldna waste sich fine words on the likes o' us. We'd like fine tae ken how it is wi' oor bairn, and maybe Sister will tell us. Ye see, we dinna understand your language.'

The great man stared at her for a moment, made a visible effort, and returned to the speech of his own boyhood.

'Well, wumman … we've tacken a' oot of his belly that suldna be there.'

'Ah, thank ye, doctor! God bless ye, doctor.'

In France a really Great Man is not cut off from the people; he feels no difficulty in talking to them. They have a kind of democracy of the mind (using democracy in the American 'idealist' sense) which we lack. This doctor in the Paris clinic was trying to share the wealth of his mind with these poor women, he was trying to explain to them what he was doing. And those slipshod assistants, in their grubby overalls, were ardent disciples, taking part in a tremendous experiment. They would have been shocked at the contemptuous way in which an English doctor regards an efficient, well-starched nurse who, he knows, will carry out to the letter treatment which she does not understand, and does not want to understand, and which he would never deign to explain to her.

In the arts the French have the same attitude. Balzac read all his novels to his cook, and I believe that once all the theatres in Paris, all the music halls and cabarets, were closed for one night so that everyone in the profession could go and see Bernhardt in *Phèdre*. Imagination boggles at such a proceeding in London. Even if we had a Bernhardt I can't believe that all our slap-stick comedians and acrobatic dancers would want to go and see her even in her greatest role. With us there is not the feeling that all the members of a profession, however humble they may be, share in the dignity and glory of its stars. This is French humanism, and I maintain that the world can't do without it.

But Magnus doesn't agree. He says the Americans have just the same kind of humanism. A Great Man over there, he says, doesn't feel cut off from simple people, and he washes his neck into the bargain. This common humanism may explain why the Americans have always got on so well with the French. I don't believe that in our time they love France because of Lafayette, or dislike Britain because of George III. There must be living contemporary reasons for these international sympathies and antipathies.

I told Mary and Magnus what David says: that Americans have their faults just as we have ours, but that tiptop Americans are the tiptop of the human race. Magnus, who is a Scot, surprised me by agreeing. And he knows Americans, for, like David, he has lived and worked in Yankeeland.

David's affection for the USA began through an episode which occurred when, as a very young man, he had a job over there. He was poor and lonely and homesick, and his rooms were so cold and cheerless that he used to spend his evenings in a public library. A girl who worked there noticed that he looked forlorn, and at last she spoke to him. When she learned that he was a stranger and lonely she asked him home to supper at her father's house. He went, and met her father, a charming and distinguished man, and so got a chance to know quite well these simple, friendly, cultured people and their circle.

✕

I asked Magnus why so many Americans dislike us. He says it is for the same reason that many other people dislike us: that we don't try to make ourselves liked, and that people consequently think us arrogant and unmatey. Magnus says history would be very different if, with our other qualities, we had a faculty for making friends.

This is true. Our manners are very bad, and we ought not to have such bad manners when we are a great nation. But how did we come to be that way? And is there any chance we may alter and improve? And would the rest of the world then like us better?

There is another point, a certain absolutely fundamental *trait* in our character which will always make us incomprehensible to other nations. It is a quality which I can only call 'unimpressionability'. We are astonishingly unimpressionable. Nothing seems to startle us or change us. We are the world's prize extroverts. We seem so incapable of any kind of impression that we appear fabulously stupid. And then we don't always behave so stupidly, so people think we must be hypocrites and insincere.

In Stacy Aumonier's book *The Golden Windmill* there is a short story called 'The Great Unimpressionable', about the adventures of an English soldier in the last war and his letters to his mother. He served on all fronts, had terrific experiences, was blown up, submarined, bombed, taken prisoner, escaped, wounded, nearly died of thirst, but all his letters are exactly the same. They are about like this: 'Dear Mother, I hope this finds you well as it leaves me. This is a funny place. The people would make you laugh to look at. We beat the 2nd Royal Scots by two goals to one. The grub is all right. How is Toffee?' (his dog). Once his mother writes that his girl is 'walkin out with another feller' and that Toffee got an ear chewed in a dog fight. He writes back: 'I was sorry about

Ettie but of course she knows what she wants I spose. You don't say what Toffee did to the other dog.'

Now I honestly think this imperviousness to impressions does offend other nations. They think we are cold and haughty, that we are refusing to be impressed, or to condescend to share an emotion, or catch our neighbour's eye and exclaim when the fireworks go off. But we aren't. We haven't *got* the emotion.

I was walking in the streets of Dublin once with a cousin when we heard a great commotion and found about two hundred people milling round a deep lock in the Canal into which a small dog had fallen. It was swimming round piteously and couldn't get out as the lock sides were steep and slimy. My cousin jumped in but had a job to get out himself, till someone threw a rope. All two hundred onlookers yelled comment and encouragement without pause and when he got up all two hundred insisted on shaking hands with him and applauded his noble deed. The Irish are the very opposite of the English. They love 'assisting' at a drama, taking part in what is going on. And I'm sure the story became epic in all the public houses in Dublin that evening.

Suppose that to happen in Lincolnshire. The crowd would have peered stolidly down at my cousin. No comment would have been made and no remarks addressed to him (he'd have got a rope, though, rather sooner than he did in Dublin). When he got up, nobody would have shaken hands with him. The crowd would have dispersed in a vague way, as if almost ashamed of having been there. And not one of them would have brightened even his wife's life by telling about it at supper.

✕

Some months ago I was in the train and I looked out of the window and saw an elephant standing in the middle of a farm yard. I was so startled that I called on all my fellow-travellers to look at the elephant. Later they all got out except one man who started talking to me. He proved to be a Czech refugee, a very nice, interesting man. Presently he asked me, very politely, if I was entirely English. I said no, my father was Irish. So he said he had thought as much. I said why? 'Because you tell us to look at the elephant. I think a lady entirely English would not have done so. Please – I admire your country so much ... ! [a great deal of politeness here, and then] ... but please, if you could explain. Would an English lady have been not surprised to see an elephant just there? Or would she have preferred to conceal her surprise?' I said *both*. It would take a vast deal to surprise an English lady, and if she was surprised she would feel no impulse to communicate her surprise to others.

He looked very despondent. And presently began: 'Deeckens! I have read already fife nofiles of Deeckens. He is so yuman. [Meaning that the English are simply *not* human.] Meesiss Yarley! Leetle Nell! Also Hamlet. You like Hamlet? He is vairy, vairy great, don't you think? And you have soch an Empire. *Soch* an Empire. Also I think you have vairy good democracy.'

These people, he felt, so utterly stupid and stodgy, incapable of surprise – how had they managed to think up Dickens and Shakespeare? How is our Empire held together? And how did we contrive to have institutions which though quaint and anachronistic do stand up to great practical strain?

I couldn't tell him. The English half of me makes me perfectly happy and at home with my fellow-countrymen. The Irish half of me makes me stand aside as an observer.

Undoubtedly we have great faults. How far we could correct them, how far any nation can at will alter its character any more than a leopard can change its spots, I don't know, but we are not a materialistic nation. Our deepest values, values which we seldom put into words but which do influence our conduct quite a lot, are spiritual and idealistic.

It is this deep unconscious sway of spiritual values which makes our people stalwart and strongly conscious of their dignity as human beings. It animates our funny old institutions and makes them into something alive and, when geared to battle, terribly tenacious and formidable.

⚹

The nine o'clock news from the Somme doesn't sound too good. There is a lot of talk about defence in depth. I hope the depth is deep enough.

5

I don't seem to have very much time for my journal with all this housework and going to bed so early.

I still cannot sleep so I went to Dr Middleton to ask for a bromide. He used to attend all our family in the old days. He asked:

'Are ye worrying about anything?'

When I said I was worrying about Hitler coming, he said, 'He won't,' so firmly that I almost believed him. He looked me up and down very crossly and said:

'I suppose ye've been reading the newspapers?'

I pleaded guilty.

'What d'ye want to do that for?'

'I like to know what is happening.'

'Aw! The newspapers don't know.'

He said if I must read a newspaper I should stick to *The Times* because I would find there any news there was put in a way that would send me to sleep instead of keeping me awake. He said that when a war broke out once in the Balkans and there were scare headlines in all the streets, *The Times* headline said: ACTIVITY IN EUROPE.

He asked me how often I listened to the wireless.

'Four times a day.'

'And that's three times too often. I'm sure I wish that infernal contrivance had never been invented. When I think of all the insanity that's poured out over the ether every minute of the day, I wonder the whole human race isn't in a lunatic asylum. And what good does it do ye to know what's happening? Ye aren't responsible. Ye don't like it. Ye can't stop it. Why think about it? Go home and fly kites with your children.'

'How many other patients have you said all this to?'

'You're only the twenty-seventh this week.'

✕

Eight hundred London school children have been evacuated to Porthmerryn. It's a comfort to know the government think this a safe corner.

Mary and Magnus were told they must take two and went down last night to the Town Hall where the children were to be allotted to their billets. All the billets had to be found in Upalong because the government, as usual, had sent someone from London to arrange it, instead of getting a local billeting officer, and Downalong wasn't taking any orders from foreigners. But that didn't mean that Downalong women were not prepared to do their bit for poor little children running away from bombs. A huge crowd of them collected outside the hall while Mary and Magnus and all the prospective hosts went inside. When the children were marched up from the railway station the women fell upon them and carried them off before ever they could get inside the hall. Each one grabbed the child of her choice with:

'You come along o' we, m'dear. I'm your new auntie.'

Now the children are all scattered to quite unexpected homes and it will take days to sort them all out. Families that were to have been kept together were separated in the turmoil, and Downalong will never let any stranger into their houses to check up on the children or inspect their sleeping quarters. It's lucky that they are certain to be kindly treated. Father Mulvaney is going to try to straighten out the muddle. He is the one common denominator in this town: a man whom everybody likes, everybody trusts, and everybody welcomes, whatever their creed or social status. Humanism?

So the Keiths came back with no Vackies after all, and are greatly relieved, for they are no longer young and rather dreaded the responsibility.

A house in our road has been turned into a hostel for children unsuitable for billets, children with contagious skin diseases, verminous children, also depraved and criminal children. It seems rather odd to put them all in one home. Good little children with pinkeye will be taught to swear and the young pickpockets will catch 'ringworm.

6

The seven o'clock news this morning was nasty.

They said that the movements of the French army are hampered by the crowds of refugees on all the roads. This is what happened in Belgium and it sounds like the beginning of the end. We were told that it wouldn't happen in France. It must mean that the Germans have got beyond the defensive zone. I said to Helga:

'Do you think that means the French are cracking?'

She said earnestly:

'If they are, the government can depend on me.'

There are worse reactions to bad news.

✕

I remember meeting a Frenchwoman at a sherry party in July, 1939. She was laughing at our ARP and our activity in training to be wardens, firefighters, etc. She said that everyone in France thought it a prime joke, and that we English seemed to be quite hysterical at the idea of war on our own soil, because we had never had to face it for such hundreds of years. But France has had it three times in seventy years, and has learnt to take it without making a fuss. There was a perceptible tinge of malice in her tone, but I thought her point was interesting. She reminded me of our old Mamselle at school, during the last war, who used to say sourly:

'You 'ave not soffer as we.'

I asked this woman if she didn't think it was a good thing for everyone to be trained and prepared.

'It appears to us,' she said, 'that you are preparing for chaos. Do you expect your people to panic?'

'Yes. If they aren't told what to do.'

'For our people that is not necessary. They are so used to it. They won't panic whatever happens.'

I knew she meant to be unpleasant, but I was impressed and felt a bit humble about it, for it is true that we have not hitherto suffered as the French have, and at that time I was inclined to believe her and suppose that the French don't need ARP as much as we do. I had the stock sentimental idea of admirable Frenchwomen refusing to be rattled by any catastrophe and ploughing fields and baking bread with battles going on all around, shrugging their shoulders and saying:

'Que voulez-vous? C'est la guerre.'

And I reminded myself that their ways are not our ways.

I saw a film just about that time in which a young French girl went out to a byre in the middle of the night and delivered a cow of a calf. She wore a longish black dress and, because the night was cold, she put over her shoulders a little white woollen shawl. And I thought how delightfully French that was. An English girl, in such an emergency, would have put on a linen overall. But I know those little shawls. Frenchwomen always put them on when they are being most admirable and clear-headed, because emergencies are so often coincident with *courants d'air*. It makes them extra feminine, but they get there just the same. I do hope they are wearing those little shawls now.

✕

Nanny's pessimism will drive me to drink. She combines it with such complacency. She has got it into her head that wishful thinking and over-confidence have landed us in this mess and that it is therefore the bounden duty of every loyal Briton to be, henceforward, as gloomy as possible. If I venture to breathe a word of hope, or even to murmur that the RAF seems to be doing rather well, she says reprovingly:

'Ah! That's how Chamberlain and Dalladeer went on.'

She seems always to be standing at the wireless, listening with a gloomy expression, beginning at 7am in her dressing gown. If it says: The Admiralty regrets to announce … she gives a sort of confirmatory groan as if to say they needn't tell her – she knew another ship had been sunk; she wouldn't be surprised if the whole navy was sunk.

✕

I feel perhaps I ought to say a word or two about old Nanny, who came back from her holiday when we came here. She is the Atlas who supports my world.

She came to me ten years ago. I didn't engage her. She engaged me. Lucy was three months old and both she and I were very ill when my rather silly little Nanny suddenly walked out announcing that the baby was going to die and she couldn't bear it. The following evening my maternity nurse, who came in to hold the fort, remarked:

'You'll be all right and so will Lucy. Nanny W has decided to come to you.'

'Who is Nanny W?' I asked.

'The best Nanny in London.'

'But she doesn't know me.'

'She has seen the children in the park and she saw you once at a children's party. She's always had a fancy to come to you. She said that little fool of a nurse wouldn't last long and she would come to you whenever you made a change. She is an exquisite needlewoman and laundress and all her nursery maids get places in titled families when she has finished training them. The last one went to Royalty. She gets them from a gamekeeper in Suffolk who has thirteen daughters and the youngest is fifteen and has just left school, Nanny W says, and is a nice girl though not so bright as her sisters, but she will do very well if Nanny W trains her, so she is coming to you too.'

'But she sounds far too grand for me.'

'Oh, she knows all about you. She knows you don't live in the style to which she has been accustomed. But she says she has always had a fancy to come to you.'

Come she did, and I have never since then had one moment of anxiety about the children. She picked up poor, pining little Lucy in her strong arms and seemed to pour all her strength and vitality into her. For two or three months the baby was never out of her arms. It is all her doing that Lucy is such a fine, healthy girl today.

But I have never been able to find out why she had a fancy to come to me, for she treats me very rough. I can seldom do or say anything right. Once she remarked to me:

'Your children were behind the door when patience was handed out.'

I said humbly that I feared their quick tempers are inherited from me.

'I know. But there's still time for *them* to learn self-control.'

She is a very shrewd, intelligent old woman with rugged, homely features. She comes from a large family in Berkshire, and she has been earning her own living since the age of thirteen, when her schooling stopped. But she is a cultured woman and has read widely. She has a very pleasant voice, and though she has far too much character to give up her native Berkshire accent, it is modulated and softened by her musical ear. She loves foreign travel and three years ago she persuaded her particular crony, Nanny S, to go with her on a trip to Paris. On their return Nanny S reported:

'We saw everything. All the History and all the Art and all the Naked Women.'

She has one foible: she will mispronounce words, especially foreign ones, and I am sure she does it on purpose. She has heard Daladier mentioned on the wireless hundreds of times, but she always calls him Dalladeer. I think she feels it is pretentious to go pronouncing foreign names too glibly.

'Dr Bench,' she said at the time of the Munich Crisis, 'knows that the Naysies won't be content with the Sunderton Lands. They'll want Alice Loring from the French and the Dodlomites from Missaloni.'

I got Benes, the Sudetenland, and the Dolomites fairly easily, but Alsace Lorraine stumped me for a long time.

7

Italy came in today. No, I won't say that. Mussolini came in today, looking for his bit of carrion. Whatever happens *he* will ultimately get his deserts. But it is very sad that we have to fight the Italians because they are nice people. Also it is awkward, as it means we have to send more ships to the Mediterranean.

Poor Magnus, who used to think so well of Mussolini, says sadly that he must have degenerated a lot since the March on Rome. I say to him:

'All power corrupts. And absolute power corrupts absolutely.'

✻

The people down here still seem to be very placid. I don't really know what they are thinking. I sit on the sand in the afternoons with a lot of other mothers, and we knit and watch our children paddling. The future of all these children, of all the children in the world perhaps, is in the balance. The magnitude of the issues is simply shattering. There has never been any moment quite like this before in the whole of history. And we sit knitting, and we have no power, *no power*, to save them from a most hideous fate. We can only wait for tomorrow.

I can imagine circumstances in which I could almost think it better to kill mine. But we don't talk about it, so I don't know if the other mothers feel that way.

Old Miss Mallaby Dixon came down today and told us all off. If we had been whimpering she would have told us to keep our chins up. As it was, she surveyed us wrathfully and said:

'You people look as if you hadn't a care in the world. Do you realise what is happening?'

Nobody said anything. We just looked at her and at our swarm of children, splashing in the surf, and it's my belief we were all sorry for her, because she hasn't any children to be terrified about. Life is an astonishing thing.

There was an American woman on the beach who is staying at one of the hotels. She has a delicate husband at home and a married daughter who lives in England and is expecting a baby shortly. She came over to be with her daughter who, I gather, is likely to have a bad time; but now her family is cabling her frantically to come back on the liner that is being sent to take Americans home, and the poor woman doesn't know whether to go or stay.

She was a natural victim for Miss Mallaby Dixon, who undertook to give a lecture on America's duty. America's duty, declared this most undemocratic of Porthmerryn's inhabitants, is to pitch in and help defend democracy. The American woman thought so, too, but I was glad and a little bit astonished at the warmth with which several other women took the opposite end of the argument. They held David's view that America came to the rescue of the European democracies once and can't be much encouraged by the result. No country can be said to have a duty to go to war unless its liberty is threatened or it is bound by solemn treaty. The question is one for America to decide for herself.

I think our warmth was partly the result of a spirit of contradiction which awakes in every bosom when the eagle nose of Miss Mallaby Dixon appears. As one of the women said later, she is, unfortunately, just the kind of Englishwoman who would be regarded by most foreigners as typical. She feels superior. Her mother was Lady Hernia Haversack, or some such person, and she never forgets it or lets others forget it.

Someone remarked that English manners get progressively worse the higher you go in the social scale. Our poor people have good manners, but they don't travel about the world, so nobody knows how nice they are, but the Mallaby Dixons travel everywhere and give us a bad name. I remarked that this wasn't true at the very top, because, by all reports, George and Bess have lovely manners. Somebody else said perhaps that is why the Americans asked them to visit last year: they had heard a rumour that we have two Britishers who know how to make themselves agreeable and they wanted to see if it was true!

This conversation interested and pleased me. It showed a kind of self-criticism of which I don't think we were capable twenty years ago. I think Magnus may be right. Perhaps we are learning.

✕

I have heard from Rhianon, who now lives on Merseyside. She is a widow. Her husband, who was everything in the world to her, died suddenly three years ago, and if she had had a smaller heart it would have been broken. But noble hearts don't break: the brittle alloy is not in them. Rhianon has lived on, outside and beyond herself, in the lives of all the people who come in contact with her and get strength and comfort from her loving warmth.

She is rather perturbed lest the people don't even now realise the ordeal that is in front of them. She knows what she is talking about, for she is in the thick of the Merseyside ARP. She trained to be a warden when David did, in May, 1938, after Hitler went into Austria, and when ARP was first started. Now she is working in a slum district and comes into contact with all sorts of people.

She says they are brave enough for anything, and will stand any amount of horrors if only they know what to expect. But she fears the first awful shock when the raids start. She thinks there may be a dangerous interval of sheer, numb stupefaction, before they pull themselves together and adapt themselves. Because neither the masses of the people nor the majority of the officials have the least idea what it will be like. They are prepared for deaths and injuries, but they seem to think that if a bomb doesn't kill or maim you life will go on quite normally. They don't envisage whole streets of homes wiped out, and huge fires, gas, water, and electric light cut off, traffic dislocated, and telephones out of order.

This mental unpreparedness is a far greater danger now than it was in 1939, because it is coupled with the invasion threat. The people may be given no time to find their feet. Those first few days of stunned shock may give Hitler his chance to get troops over.

I get the same account from Claire's parents in London. They say all the preparations there seem to be made in the expectation that everyone will shortly be dead. In the hospital where they are living there are thirty thousand cardboard coffins all folded flat, stacked up, and waiting for occupants. And there are acres of trench graves already dug.

A dead Londoner will be wonderfully catered for. So will an injured Londoner. The medical services are well organised, the ambulances and first-aid posts are all ready, there is plenty of hospital accommodation, and supplies of blood are kept ready for transfusion. But a homeless Londoner is going to be out of luck, though there will surely be many more of them than of dead or wounded.

Anna says the same thing. She says there should be emergency feeding centres, hostels, and clothing depots. But hardly any preparations of that kind are being made. She talked to an official in an East End district and he actually said:

'People from a bombed house can go into a neighbour's.'

Anna pointed out that one bomb can demolish a street. There might be no neighbours. Want of imagination is the curse of this country. Everything that has been foreseen has been very efficiently provided for, but our preparations seem to be a mixture of superb organisation and purblind muddle.

Far too much, Anna says, is being left to local authorities. They are often genial woolly-headed old duffers, elected because they are popular in the district and quite capable of fixing a water-rate or deciding where the new recreation ground is to be, but they hardly know the difference between a high explosive and an incendiary bomb and will be about as useful in Armageddon as a popgun.

The government is still refusing to provide deep shelters. Their idea is to disperse the population, so that no one bomb shall have a chance of falling on a large collection of people. Also they probably fear panic among people pushing and crowding down staircases and narrow passages. That sounds all right. But people who went through it in Barcelona say that nothing will check the urge to burrow down underground, especially at night. The people may actually be safer in their Anderson huts but they won't feel safer. However undesirable deep shelters may be, the public will insist on having them, so it is a pity not to start making them now. If they are not there, the people will creep down into any old holes and sewers, and all sorts of epidemics will break out, and the situation get really out of hand. This is what Anna says, anyway. But her informants are mostly Communists who fought in the Spanish War, and they think everything done by the government is wrong.

It's astonishing how many people still seem to think there will be no big bombing, simply because we have not had any yet. And fantastic things are asserted about the efficacy of our anti- aircraft defences. It is widely said that no enemy bomber will ever reach London. Time and time again people have said to me, quite confidently:

'You know what the RAF say? They say the Germans will come to London *once*.'

Rhianon says she cheers herself up by watching the soldiers rehearsing invasion tactics in Birkenhead Park, assisted by all the little boys in the neighbourhood.

8

Paris has fallen.

Or perhaps I should say Paris has been given away with a pound of tea. First we were told that it would be defended to the last brick; then that the defence of Paris was not an isolated battle and that it is a bastion in Weygand's line (whatever that is); then that it was an open town and would not be defended at all.

The French government has gone to Tours. Reynaud says they will fight on in the provinces, in one province only, in Africa, but they will never give in. I wonder if he has enough Frenchmen behind him. They are, they can be, a most heroic nation. It seems like disloyalty to them, in their suffering, to start giving up hope.

But the Germans are in Paris! I can't believe it. Those barbarian hordes have trampled down that lovely, lovely city. Hitler, who has never been anywhere or seen anything outside Hunland, who wouldn't know a civilised city if he saw one – he will ride in now as a conqueror, I suppose. Oh, if I had been French, I would rather have seen Paris bombed to little bits! I would far rather see dear old London bombed to little bits than let those apes set foot in it.

✕

'Now, Margaret! Not apes. Not all of them apes. Remember that Hitler did not get a majority vote from the German people, even after the Reichstag fire. If they were all apes there would be no need for Dachau. Try to be a good European.'

'Silly cows, then, to put up with Hitler if they don't really want him. It's worse to be a fool than a knave, because a knave can reform and a fool can't. And anyway it's the Nazis I'm calling apes.'

'It's not a peculiarly German ape. There are gangsters in every country. Certain conditions might put them on top in any country. If France goes down there will be nuts for French apes. If we go down there will be nuts for apes everywhere. Don't be sidetracked into the ape-like habit of hating 'the Germans'. Beware of fighting monsters lest you yourself become a monster.'

'Oh, it's too tough! I can't fight and not hate. I can't see my children in deadly peril and not want to make soup of the Germans.'

'What have you a religion for then? Get down on your knees and pray for grace to be a good European. You aren't sure if it's right to pray for Victory but you can always pray for grace.'

✕

This is the sort of conversation I am always having with my Guardian Angel.

✕

We feel already as if we had been living here for months. In this nightmare all days seem alike, and one loses all sense of time.

The worst news seems to come through on the 1pm bulletin. We hear this down at the hotel it where we have luncheon. The wireless is in the sun lounge. We sit with the residents in a circle of cane chairs, listening, and then shuffle silently into the dining room. There is almost no conversation during the meal at any of the tables. The children exchange bored glances. Grown-ups going on and on about it were bad enough; grown-ups who don't talk at all are infinitely worse.

The three girls never talk about the war or ask how things are going. They have put up a defensive barrage of bored indifference. I don't know how far their sense of security may be shaken below the surface, but none of them shows any of the little signs indicative of nervous disturbance.

Charles takes too much interest. He constantly asks if 'the war has got to London' and if his father is quite safe. He was terribly distressed because he heard somebody say that France would probably make a separate peace.

'I thought France liked us so much,' he said dolefully. 'And I never knew that countries broke their promises.'

He is fascinated by the idea of Hitler. The other day, when he had been scolded for something, he walked down Fore Street in Porthmerryn giving the Nazi salute and shouting:

'Heil Hitler! I shall do all the wairst things in the wairld. Heil Hitler!'

As though he had taken service with the Devil.

It's odd that we don't dream of Hitler. One would have thought we should have nightmares about him all the time. But I have asked everyone I know, and they all say no, they don't dream of him at all. Perhaps it is because our fears are no longer suppressed.

I have had no war dreams since May. Before that I often dreamt that we had a gas alarm and I put the children's masks on and found that all the nozzles had vanished. Obviously some kind of frustration dream – a consciousness of being unprepared.

The other night I had a vivid dream that I was a steam roller. I was bowling along a road at a great pace with Viola and Rhianon, and we were all chattering and gossiping. They were steam rollers too. Presently Rhianon said:

'Look, we are taking up far too much room. If a car came round the corner there would be a smash. We ought to go in single file.'

So Viola went on ahead, close to the hedge, and I followed, and Rhianon brought up the rear, and we rumbled along in silence. At last I looked back and said:

'This is a bore. We can't talk anymore.'

To which she replied:

'We must take thought for others, my dear.'

She was a steam roller except for her head, where the funnel should have been, and her face was twenty years younger, not the wise, calm face it is now, but the face she had when we were girls at college, round, merry, dimpled; and all her magnificent red hair streamed away in the wind as it used to do before she shingled it years and years ago.

9

Now the worst has happened. Reynaud is going to ask for an armistice. He says that France cannot go on. He seems to have made some appeal to President Roosevelt. I can't see what is the good of that. What could Roosevelt do? But perhaps Reynaud was playing for time. Or perhaps it the French government want to justify themselves for giving up: 'The other democracies can't or won't help us, so why should we fight alone?'

Magnus and I heard the news at 9pm. Magnus made a queer little noise: 'Er-er-er!' As if something had broken inside him.

Afterwards we heard somebody, I think it was Vernon Bartlett, but I was so flustered it might have been anybody, who told us that it is quite all right because we still have the French fleet which is the second finest fleet in the world. Oh, is *that* so? I think I see Hitler signing an armistice while we still have the French fleet. If he has got the French people in his power he will torture them till they give it up.

After the news I rang David up in London. I felt that I must hear his voice. He was unexpectedly cheerful. He is not often more optimistic than I am. He says he doesn't think for a moment that the French will give up their fleet to Hitler.

Rather than do anything so dishonourable they will continue to fight in Africa.

10

Reynaud has resigned. Old Pétain is taking over. Good grief! He is eighty-three! I don't know what to make of the new French government. They all seem to be soldiers and sailors. Does that mean they will go on fighting? No, I don't think so. When the soldiers take over it is always a bad sign. And Mandel is out; he was a solid *jusqu'au boutist*.

Winston says it makes no difference. We shall go on. Thank God for that. It seems that we made a last-minute offer of a 'solemn act of union with France'. Pity we didn't do this before. And why solemn? Are such things usually accomplished in a slap-and-tickle atmosphere?

O God, I wish we knew what is going to happen to the French fleet.

✖

I met Mrs Harkness, an Upalong matron, on the hill this morning. She looked very brisk and cheerful in her good, expensive tweeds and sensible shoes, and her white hair curling crisply all over her head. She asked if there was any news. I said only the news about France.

'What about France? Our wireless has gone wrong and I never seem to get time to read the paper.'

'France is out of the war.'

'What?'

'She is asking for an armistice.'

'France is? *France*? But why?'

'They say they can't go on.'

'But … how queer! How very strange! I must say that does surprise me. I always thought that France …'

She paused, as if not quite sure what it was she had always thought about France. Then she sighed and said:

'I ought to read the papers more.'

She is very busy with her Vackies. She had been put down for two, but when they came she found that they were pining for their younger brother and sister, so she offered to take all four. They are Anny, aged twelve, Ireen, aged ten, Sheila, aged eight, and Duncan, aged five. They are charming children and come from a terribly poor home. The only trouble she had was getting them to go to bed early. At home they stayed up till their parents went to bed, as the whole family lives in one room. They evidently complained of the early hours when they wrote home, for they brought her a letter from 'our Mum' to read, and Mum said: 'Do not fret about early bed. Sleep is very good for children if people can afford it. The lady is giving you all of her best.'

Sleep is good if people can afford it.

Oh, sometimes I think our civilization is not worth saving.

11

Lucy is practising the piano. She is playing scales very carefully and slowly. Her braids fall on either side of the little white triangle at the back of her neck. There is nothing in the world softer, or whiter, or more tender than the back of a little girl's neck.

I can't bear it. Why did I bring her into the world? If Hitler wins they had much better be dead. All that they are, all that I have taught them and tried to instil into them, all their innocence and promise, would only become an extra cause of suffering to them.

Always before, in any trouble or anxiety, they have been an unfailing source of consolation. Now I can hardly bear to look at them. They are a sword in my heart.

12

David and Claire's father are here. They have rushed down to consult me about sending the children to Canada. They both think that we ought to go on fighting, but they think our number is up and they want to get the children out. Claire's father thinks he can pull strings to get them off quickly.

David and I don't feel quite happy about pulling strings. There is talk of a government scheme for evacuating children overseas and I would be willing to put them down for that, perhaps, though I choke when I think of the risks of the voyage. Still, I suppose the risks of staying here are worse.

But I think we must be careful to act quite rightly. 'Devil take the hindmost' is a dangerous motto. However extensive the government scheme may be, it is obvious that the great mass of our children can't go. We must not ask others to endure what we are not able to face ourselves. There must be absolute equality and fairness of opportunity about this thing, otherwise we shall have class bitterness. The Harkness Vackies mean exactly as much to their Mum as my three do to me, and they ought to have an equal chance of safety.

Claire's father is haunted by Poland, the awful things the Germans are doing there and the thought that they will do as bad, and worse, if they get here. I know. I know. But Reynaud said, at the beginning of the Battle for France, that the issue depended on each one 'doing his duty with ferocious determination'. And that meant civilians as well as soldiers. We must put duty before everything now. The fate of all children may depend, just a little bit, on what we do with ours. I am for waiting till we hear more about the government scheme. It needs ferocious determination to say it, though.

David is inclined to agree with me, but he says we don't know from day to day what may happen. There might be some kind of mass immigration arranged. He wants me to get our passports and immigration papers in order, even mine and Nanny's, so as to be ready for any event. To do that much would not tie us to any decision, and I have agreed to see to it.

✕

Nanny says an Abbess is threatening to swallow the whole of Europe.

✕

The news from France gets worse in every bulletin. It seems to be complete capitulation. We don't know the terms yet but our people keep rushing to Bordeaux as if they were trying to prevent some terrible catastrophe. It is generally accepted now that we have not got the French fleet; the only question is whether Hitler will get it. Pétain declares that the French will never accept dishonourable terms. In crises they always begin to talk about their honour, but Magnus says their idea of honour is peculiar, and consists simply of looking after themselves. He says they would think it a blot on their honour to give up an inch of French territory but would hand over their neighbour's goods without sneezing.

A look at the map is enough to make one wish one had never learnt geography. All the French Mediterranean Sea bases gone, and the armies in Algeria and Syria, which should have protected our flanks in Egypt, gone too.

And the French called Leopold a traitor for going out!

We all have the most acute pains in our stomachs. It feels as if most of our organs had been removed.

But there is just one aspect of the matter which we must never forget. Barring certain gangsters in every country, who hope to get pickings, there is nobody in the world who wants Hitler to win. In no nation do the people want to see a Nazi-dominated Europe. The Italians don't. The Russians don't.

The Spaniards don't. The Americans don't. I shouldn't be surprised if the Germans don't.

This is the truth, and it may yet bring Hitler's downfall. The nations of the world may not altogether like the British Empire, but in resisting Nazi tyranny we are truly representing the will of the whole civilised world. That will is not effective yet. It is crushed and silenced and hampered everywhere. But if we exert ourselves to the utmost and endure all, perhaps we can hang on till means are found to make that will effective.

This must be our hope. It is a real hope. It shines like a tiny beacon across a waste of terror and desolation. But every month, every week, day, hour, and minute that we manage to hold on brings it that much nearer. Every day will show the world more clearly what Nazism really is, and open the eyes of those who are still blind, and convince people that any sacrifice is better than submission. Every day will convince more Americans that we are worth helping, and that this battle is vital to their own safety. When they see that, they will find ways of helping us. Every day will teach the subject populations better how to resist. Unrest and sabotage will grow. Hitler's armies will be menaced by a fifth column far larger and more effective than he ever dreamed of. Europe will never be more submissive than she is today, and America will never be more isolationist. And every single blow we strike, every pang we endure, will help, as long as we remain the rallying point of world resistance.

All history tells us that we have a chance if only we can hold on.

13

Today we all went for a walk along the cliffs. I have never seen the coast look lovelier. The sea was like a peacock's wing, vivid blue and green with purple shadows. It was very calm and washed round the granite rocks with scarcely a plume of spray. I have never looked upon such beauty before without my heart leaping up. But today my heart stayed in my stomach and I watched the waves and realised that, like Coleridge,

I *see*, not *feel*, how beautiful they are.

It's all very well for Wordsworth to say that Nature never did betray. I don't believe he was ever as frightened as I am.

We sat on a headland, looking out over the sea. The poor children scuffled round us like disconsolate puppies. They had thought their fathers' visit would be a glorious bean feast, but now they are disillusioned.

Claire's father says he will try to go to Canada if Hitler wins, and carry on his surgical research there. He was just on the track of tremendous things when war broke out.

David says he will stay here and try to organise revolt, and get shot. If he tries this, I shall have to help him with it. We shall make the world's worst conspirators.

Claire's father takes a gloomy view of the future of the USA if Hitler wins. He says it doesn't matter how fast they re-arm, they will be betrayed from within. He says nothing succeeds like success, and if democracy goes down in Europe a lot of noodles will begin to admire Hitler; the workers will be encouraged to believe that they will get more if they sacrifice their freedom, and the rich will be told that they are being saved from Communism. He quoted Sinclair Lewis' *It Can't Happen Here* and John Steinbeck's *The Grapes of Wrath*.

But I say it is not fair to judge America from the novels of Lewis or Steinbeck who are remorseless critics of their own country. What takes Lewis' imagination is dissonance; he is interested in paradoxes and discrepancies. What is fine and noble he does not bother to mention – perhaps because he and his public take it for granted as part of the air they breathe. Willa Cather or Dorothy Canfield gives an entirely different picture but quite as true. If American democracy were put to the test wouldn't the people they write about carry the day rather than the people Lewis and Steinbeck write about?

It's funny to be so worried about American freedom. But I do want to feel that democracy is safe somewhere.

14

It was only a short visit. Both the men went back tonight so as to be at work tomorrow morning. After I had seen them off I went up to the Keiths' and we heard the terms of the French armistice on the 9pm news bulletin.

They are just about as bad as they can be. There is a pretence that the fleet won't be handed over, but I feel sure it will. Half of France, including Paris, is to be occupied, and none of the French prisoners are to be released until we will consent to leave off fighting. This is obviously designed to make the French hate us.

Hitler means to make everything quite intolerable for everyone, everywhere, and then point to us as the villains of the piece. In neutral countries this may have some success. It will have none in any place where there are Germans. No need to tell Poland, Czecho-Slovakia, Denmark, Holland, Belgium, or northern France, why we are going on. The Nazis themselves are the best anti-Nazi propaganda.

I suppose we expected it, but it came as a terrible shock. Magnus gave one look at Mary and me, got up, and stumped out of the house. Mary knelt by the wireless and murmured:

'This isn't the end. This is only the beginning.'

She stared in front of her, with a faraway expression in her lovely eyes, as if she was looking at something not yet made plain.

She went upstairs, I think to cry, and I profited by my solitude to bellow heartily. Presently she came back with a whisky decanter and we both had a stiff one. Then Magnus came in, very cross. It seems that he had been off to volunteer for the Home Guard and was told he is too old. He is seventy-four but nobody would think it. Mary flew into a fine rage and said how could he think of such a thing, climbing about the cliffs with a gun in the middle of the night with his rheumatism? But I know how he feels. He just must try to defend his women.

I am glad I went through this blackest hour with them.

15

Helga has got a new god to worship. She has got a picture of a French general pinned up over her mantelpiece. He is General de Gaulle, who is in London and says he will not give up, and is calling on all Frenchmen to join him. It seems that he is a tank expert, so I suppose he is the general Beryl told me about, whose name I thought was Géle.

He may not count for much, or he may turn out something tremendous, but he is the first fruits of our determination to fight on.

Winston says we are going to restore France in all her glory. Even if we could beat Hitler, we couldn't do that. Glory isn't a brown paper parcel that one nation can make a present of to another. If France wants her glory back she must get it for herself, Poland, Norway, Holland, and Belgium never lost theirs; they did not break their word, though *they* were invaded. But De Gaulle keeps the torch alight. At the very least he is useful as a symbol. Helga worships him with mystic ardour. She says he is *le grand celtique* who will, according to Nostradamus, overcome Anti-Christ. He is the True France.

There are endless rumours about the French, their colonies, and their fleet. Porthmerryn is full of people who know someone who was in Plymouth yesterday and saw hundreds of French battleships. Many French politicians are said to be on the way here, but on the other hand many may think it their duty to stay in France and even make pleasant faces at Hitler for a while in the hope of hampering the machinations of French Quislings. Where France and Frenchmen are concerned we must suspend judgment till we know all the truth. It is difficult not to feel bitter, but we must remember what they are suffering.

✳

I can't really take it all in. The catastrophe is too colossal. The future is too terrifying. The issues, for the whole world, are too tremendous. I can't believe it is really all happening. But I am glad that I have read so much history. Partly because everything I ever read leads me to hope. Partly because it helps one to keep sane to remember that all this is only a paragraph in that

> ... ample page
> Rich with the spoils of Time ...

But there is one thing I never fully grasped before: that every word in the ample page is written in human blood and human tears.

16

So now there is only duty that we can be sure of. Because we can never be quite in despair as long as we feel we have a duty – as long as one course seems, ideally, more worth pursuing than another. That means that our faith still stands and our ideas of right and wrong, foul and fair, just and unjust, are still unshaken. Where faith survives, hope survives, for faith is the substance of things hoped for.

✳

This afternoon I took the Untouchables from the Hostel down to the beach. I tied up my hair in a handkerchief and put on a cotton overall, and a good thing too, for among them they have apparently got:

Ringworm, pinkeye, itch, scab, and impetigo.

What else they have got I would rather not know. I took a lysol bath as soon as I got home.

There were twenty of them, the eldest fourteen and the youngest four, but they were easy to amuse for they only wanted to jump up and down and yell. If somebody had given them a tom-tom they would have been perfectly happy. Matron said I was not to let them paddle, so I ran up and down on the edge of the sea like a collie, herding them away from it. They did not care to make sandcastles. I had some old golf balls and built them a balliechute, but they were only mildly interested, and after watching the balls go down the track once they went back to their war dance.

One wizened little boy with a shaven head was an exception. He was enchanted with it and played with it all the afternoon, making the most ingenious improvements. He made a double track so that two golf balls could go down at once, one running in a series of tunnels under the other. His great object was to get them to go down at equal speed, so that both started and finished together.

Just as he had got it, a little devil called Len deliberately jumped on it and destroyed it, shouting derisively:

'Crabs! Crabs!'

The gnome said nothing, but patiently started to build it up again. Len jumped on it again, and howled with agony, for sharp-edged pieces of slate had been buried in the sand on purpose for his bare feet. The gnome's name is Aloysius. He should go far. It isn't often that the creative temperament has so much instinct for self-protection.

Reeny, a freckled redhead with a grin that was almost friendly, was the most communicative. She told me they mostly come from Stepney. During the first months of the war they were evacuated to Suffolk. I asked what it was like in Suffolk.

'Rotten,' said Reeny briefly.

'What was wrong with it?'

'A bee stang me.'

'How long were you there?'

'Ight munce.'

'When did the bee sting you?'

'Larst di fore I come 'ere.'

There was no other accusation against Suffolk. The food was OK and the school was OK and the lidy was everserkind and asked Mum to stay at Christmas. But a bee stang her on the last day and so Suffolk was rotten.

That is the worst of children. They have no sense of the present continuous; they can only answer for the moment. It is never any use to ask them if they are happy. They don't know.

She told me that poor Aloysius had crab lice and that is why his head is shaved and all the others shout 'Crabs' at him.

'All us kids is supposed to have somethink wrong wiv us,' she explained cheerfully.

It was on the way home that I got into trouble. I took them up the cliff path, which crosses the railway cutting by a foot-bridge and then goes up in zigzags, among rocks and brambles and blackthorn, and in sheltered spots there are benches. Halfway up I missed the awful Len. Then I saw that he had scrambled to a rocky pinnacle and was rolling down boulders onto the heads of people below. I yelled to him to stop. He took not the slightest notice. So I scrambled up to his pinnacle, using language which I am sure he never hears from Matron, and which seemed almost to quell him for a moment, I think with surprise. But when I looked down I saw that, in just two minutes, all the nineteen others had got into some kind of trouble. Reeny had fallen down and hurt her knee. Several boys had got onto another pinnacle and were rolling stones down in imitation of Len. Lil and Ireen had got into some stinging nettles and were howling loudly. Some more were being frightened by a big dog. A lot had managed to get through the wire fence onto the railway line. And the rest had simply disappeared.

Kind people were rushing from all directions to pick them up, and pull them down, and bind them up, and frighten the dog off, and snatch them from under the wheels of the 4.30 train which was due at any moment round the corner. The air was loud with indignant demands for 'the person in charge.'

O me! My duty!

Chapter Four

July: 'We're Not So Green As We're Cabbage-Looking'

1

Mme Tabouis, the French journalist who always knows everything, says that Hitler has declared he will dictate a world peace from Buckingham Palace on July 15. If he said that, which I don't quite believe, he must have been reckoning on our throwing up the sponge when France collapsed. For he hasn't begun his invasion yet.

One would have thought he'd have come the day the French armistice was signed. But perhaps the Battle for France went even quicker than he expected, so that his preparations for invasion have not quite reached the stage he meant them to be at when France finally went down. Also he may not have reckoned on the RAF turning out so well, or on our having the army back from Dunkirk to defend us. All those things may explain this pause.

Some people think he will have a terrific air blitz first and try to knock out the RAF before he attempts troop landings. Others say he will go for Eire next, so as to surround us completely and cut off our Atlantic sea routes. It would be awkward for us if he did that, so we hope he won't, but if he does we shan't be one little bit sorry for the Irish. A taste of the Nazis would open their eyes, after all the song and dance they have made about English oppression. And the Nazis wouldn't find it all jam, either. They would have an ostensible walkover, of course, if once they landed troops. They could occupy the whole island while De Valera was dressing his troops up in twelfth-century costume and deciding what was the authentic battle cry of Brian Boru. But afterwards, a surprising lot of the invaders would get murdered. In fact I should almost be sorry for the Huns.

✕

We went into Penmorvah today for a medical inspection – the first step towards getting our immigration papers in order. They are now putting up barriers on these roads, just as they were doing in Surrey last month. There is only a very small gap in the middle, so that cars have to crawl through at walking pace; and there are two or three round, barrel-shaped blocks of concrete, all ready to roll into the gap, if orders should come to close it. I notice that these barriers generally occur at corners, and always where there is a coppice or high wall by the road, which can conceal a gun post.

There are no soldiers to be seen anywhere, but the bus driver said there is a large force of troops quite near by, he is not at liberty to say where.

The doctor was an aged and vague individual who took hours to make the most perfunctory examination. He filled up lots of forms in a haphazard way, and put Charles down as pregnant. I couldn't help protesting at that. The MO pondered for a long while but eventually agreed with me so far as to put *male*, in brackets, after the word pregnant.

Ellen's sight, with and without glasses, stumped him completely. First he spent half an hour searching for a book which, when found, turned out to be in French, and gave all measurements in metres and centimetres. Then he held up letters for Ellen to read, with and without glasses. Then he got a tape-measure and started to crawl about on the floor, measuring distances. But as he had by then forgotten where he was standing and she was standing when she read the letters, it was rather like the game of croquet in *Alice in Wonderland*. So then he had to start all over again while Nanny and I crawled about the floor with the tape-measure. And then he had to do hours and hours of sums, turning inches into centimetres and back again. In the end he came to the conclusion that she could see twice as well without glasses as with, which would worry me had it not been obvious, when she was reading the letters off, that this was not the case.

He was a nosy old Parker too, and asked a lot of questions about things which didn't concern him. There was a lot of pausing and puffing and blowing over Claire whom he clearly suspected of being illegitimate, my child by another father.

By the time he got to me and Nanny he was quite exhausted and ready to call it a day. I don't suppose he had put in so much work for ten years. He asked Nanny if she was pregnant. Perhaps he has read his Bible and knows what happened to Sarah. I was the only member of the party he did not ask about this, although I am the only one it could apply to. He merely asked me if I had any relatives in a lunatic asylum and signed me off as medically fit.

But I am getting more and more sure we shan't go. The government scheme hangs fire and already there are murmurs about how influential people are rushing their children out. I know of several who have got theirs off already. On the other hand, David has discussed the whole question with various friends in London and found that many take our view of the situation and are not going to do anything in a hurry. The Sorleys, for instance, who are very rich and have relatives in America, are keeping their children here because they think we must at all costs avoid anything that seems like a panic rush, and that our first duty is to keep up morale. John Sorley says firmly that all shipping accommodation available for this purpose should be commandeered by the government and that there should be no private evacuation.

Still, I would never say that any given family did wrong to send its children. Circumstances make the ethics of each case so different. Some children are far less able than others to stand the life over here.

I discussed it with some of the mothers on the beach. One woman took the line that no duty can come higher than a mother's duty to her children, and that the State should not require her to do anything prejudicial to her children's lives. There is no higher law. So we asked this: supposing she were wrecked with a lot of children, some hers and some not, and the food supplies ran low, would she starve the other children so as to keep all the food for her own? She thought for a bit and then said no, she would share out the food among all the children alike. So she does recognise a higher law. In moments of great emergency it has got to be: Each mother for all children.

✖

The expensive hotels are filling up with expensive evacuées. We call them the Gluebottoms because they seem able to do nothing but sit. In the lounges and on the beaches you find them in hammock chairs, complaining of the personal inconvenience to which this war has put them. Most of them are elderly women, but quite a few are young and able-bodied. They play golf and bridge, expect a large staff of servants to be kept to wait on them, and say that there is nothing to do in Porthmerryn. Meanwhile the residents are looking after eight hundred Vackies, haymaking, training for Home Guard, fire fighting, and ARP, and digging for victory. Do these broad-beamed women really imagine the nation is facing all this to keep them sitting pretty?

✖

(January 25, 1941, 10.30pm. It's queer to think of those quiet July days now, while I am typing this out to send to the USA for

safekeeping. Something very noisy is going on, and the house keeps waving about. The children are on a mattress under the kitchen table, looking like a basket of goslings. Charles says he doesn't mind bangs as long as he is not parted from his sisters. Nanny is making tea and I have been reading them The Magic Shop. *We shall have to do something about a shelter if this sort of thing goes on. A Hun bomber keeps zoomzazoomzazooming away across the bay and then keeps coming back. But we seem to be having a lull and I have gone back to typing out my journal. Lord Halifax has arrived in the* USA *and an Aussie tin hat has replaced the Top Wop's flag in Tobruk. And we are still waiting for this here invasion. But this is not an 'experiment in time' so I had better go back to July, 1940.)*

2

We are all bidden to a series of lectures on ARP.

Porthmerryn has never bothered about such a thing before. But now we are waking up. I went down to the Town Hall with Mary and Magnus and we were told all about gas, high explosive, and incendiary bombs. It was the sort of thing everybody in London knew at latest by September, 1938, but it is a novelty here. Even now I could see no Downalong at the lecture, probably because the course has been organised by Upalong.

Mr Trelawney, the chemist, spoke first. He told us, in his mild, hesitating voice, that he believed the official air raid advice is that resentment is a good antidote to fear. 'If you find yourself frightened in a raid,' he said, 'you should try to feel resentment.' So we all wrote down in our books: (1) Keep away from windows. (2) Corner of room better than middle. (3) Feel resentment.

In order to protect the ear drums, he said, the mouth should be lightly closed and the teeth left open. Everybody made the most peculiar faces when they practised this. I'm sure I should never remember. *(January 25, 1941: One doesn't. I haven't done it all evening.)*

Colonel Farraday, looking very cheerful, showed us how to work a stirrup pump and advised us all to get one, adding that there are none to be had anywhere just now. He also explained how to put up an Anderson steel shelter and said that none were being issued in this part of the country. He then showed us how to put out an incendiary bomb with sand and a long-handled shovel. He told us how he had been gassed in the last war, and that cheered us all up tremendously, for it had not occurred to us that anyone could be gassed and live to tell the tale, much less tell it as zestfully as Colonel Farraday. Finally he invited us to become wardens and said anybody could be one – 'men, or women, or clergymen' – which provoked us to unseemly giggles.

✕

(January 25, 1941. Later. After a lull there is a sudden rattle of machine-gunning, so I leave my typing and go back to the kitchen to see how the family is getting on. Nanny says it is simply 'fertile' to attack a little place like this. The children have been asleep, but the machine-gunning roused them and they are squabbling drowsily.

Lucy is airing all her grievances. She has launched into one of her long diatribes, describing, first, all the impossible tasks she is expected to perform and, secondly, all the disadvantages which an unfair world has put upon her. The fact that she drops her g's and can't say her r's makes it all the more impressive.

'It's widiculous! I'm s'posed to learn my Bach piece as far as bar sixteen by Monday, and I shall be a weck tomorrow with this wetched waid keepin' me awake. I don't think a person ought to be expected to do it.'

Ellen: 'It's ridiculous you starting to play Bach when you can't even spell.'

Lucy: 'Spellin's got nothin' to do with music.'

Ellen: 'When I was your age I wasn't allowed to play Bach.'

Lucy: 'You aren't now. You have to play silly ole Beethoven.'

Ellen: 'You don't play proper Bach. Only Bach arranged for the Tiny Tots.'

Lucy: 'I do not.'

Charles: 'Oh shut you chewdren and let a feller get some sleep.'

✳

Claire says nothing. She lies on her back, her grey eyes wide open, and stares meditatively at the lamp. I don't know what her thoughts may be. Lying there in the dim light she looks heart-rendingly like her dead mother.

Grief, shock and loss have put a gulf between her and the other three. They face life with a careless, untried confidence which she has lost. Silly fools write to me and say they are sure I will be a second mother to her. There is, there can be, no such thing. The most I can be is a friend. My heart aches to see her lying there, so young, so tender, so valiant, gazing forlornly out on a bleak and brutal world. That look of hers shatters me more than the bombs do. Again a lull. Again a return to my journal of last summer.)

✳

July, 1940. I have done all that we have been told to do. I have ordered a stirrup pump, and bought a long-handled shovel and a bucket for sand. I have pasted net over the windows as a protection against glass splinters. I have got a lot of first-aid appliances, including tannic acid for burns, and put them on the gas-mask shelf. I have taught the children what to do if caught in the open. And they now play a horrible game which they call practising. One of them suddenly makes an ear-splitting noise, which they say is a whistling bomb, and the others fall flat on their faces, their hands over their ears, teeth open, mouths lightly closed.

I was pleased the other day to find out how well they have learned these things, and how little they mind the bangings we sometimes have to hear. We were out in the fields when we heard a series of explosions. We thought it was a raid, but it turned out only to be something being blown up in defence preparations. I was much reassured by their behaviour. They all did the right things, and Charles remarked calmly: 'Is that Hitler makin' that shockin' noise? Thank goodness I've got me gas mask!'

If we aren't occupied and they don't get bombed or badly undernourished, they will do very well. They are happy and gay and full of life and hope and spirit. I don't think the war has hurt them yet. But for all that I have moments when I long to get them away.

Helga thinks people go much too far with raid precautions. In her bathroom she has put a small sugar-basin full of sand and a trowel – her gesture towards a bucket and long-handled shovel. 'I shall do no more than that,' she announces, 'not if they come and fling me into prison.'

She is working in the scullery at the Hostel and enjoying it greatly, for the Vackies are much more wicked than anyone in Upalong or Downalong and Helga finds them entertaining. They have broken into several houses and all wrote home to their parents to say that this place had been bombed to bits and that most of the children here have been killed. This brought a rush of panic-stricken parents down to take them away. Len, who rolled the boulders down the cliff, seems to be the ringleader. He was sent away to a special home for uncontrollable children, near Penmorvah, but after three days he was returned because he had made the principal cry. So now Father Mulvaney has offered to take him.

Nanny and I help with the washing and mending at the Hostel. Today I sewed a button on a little shirt that had come, according to the tab inside, from R H Macy, New York. I wonder how many vicissitudes it has seen before it found its way to a Rotherhithe slum home. It is a good shirt, hardly worn at all. Americans are sending over a lot of clothes for children. This must have come in one of the bundles. Some mother sent it because she was sorry for our children. And now, if we can hold the pass, she won't ever have to be frightened for her children in the way we are for ours.

3

The hateful suspense over the French fleet has been relieved in a way that is scarcely less hateful. We have sunk or damaged a large part of it at Oran. Everyone is feeling sick with mingled relief and disgust. I fear this wretched episode will lie between us and the French for all time.

Winston spoke well about it, as usual. Skillfully gauging the feelings of the nation, he told us something that helped us to swallow the nauseating pill. He said that when France capitulated the Bordeaux government returned to Germany four hundred Nazi airmen who were our prisoners, whom our pilots had shot down while they were bombing and machine-gunning French civilians. Without any reference to us, these fliers were set free to come back and bomb us. That the French should leave us to our fate is one thing; that they should actually be willing to help Hitler against us – their allies of last month – is another. We never asked that their fleet should be handed over to us; only that it should be put where Hitler could not get it.

It's all a devilish trick. France has been stunned, knocked senseless, and a hideous *Doppelgänger* has been conjured up in her place. It is as if some gracious, beautiful woman, a queen, had been outraged by savages. It is an unclean horror that cannot be talked about or thought of. It is not tragedy. It has not the dignity of tragedy. No poet in after ages will want to write on such a theme.

I'm glad they have banned the Marseillaise. I'm glad it is now De Gaulle's song. I remember the end of *Boule de Suif* and how those base, sordid people hated to hear the man whistling it in the coach. 'The song of the people'.

✖

The news from Oran has made me feel sadder and more desolate than ever. Just because our own danger is a little less the tragedy of Europe comes more into the foreground. The triumph of evil is so overwhelming – this distortion of men and nations out of their natural selves.

Only the children are pleased about Oran. I heard two of them playing at being Hitler informed by Goebbels of what had happened.

'Bring me my carpet that I may bite it.'

'Which flavour, mein Führer?'

'Lemon, Joe. And I'll have a nibble at the raspberry rug.'

✖

In Verona on a hot summer night the people pulled their kitchen tables out into the street in front of the houses and sat at supper there. The tall, plain old houses stood up like fortresses against the deep night sky, and the doorways were little caves of light. And families sat round the scrubbed wooden tables before the doorways, and the food on the tables was simple and gracious and shapely – Chianti in long-necked bottles, and great loaves, orange-coloured cheese, tawny sausages, and grapes and figs. And the fine, muscular men sat in their shirt-sleeves, tired and at repose, and the women in their black shawls moved in and out of the lighted kitchens. And there was nothing in the whole scene that was not simple and essential, but at the same time beautiful and satisfying to see.

They have a very old civilisation. They knew how to live, they were living very much like this when our ancestors were painting themselves with woad. They make our northern way of life seem uncouth and ugly. English working people have a far higher standard of life, but they don't know so well what to do with it.

Now we call the Italians the Wops, and think of them as a lot of swarthy little men dressed up in uniform and drafted off to sandy deserts where, if we are successful in cutting off their water supplies, they may perish horribly of thirst. But it is their nature to sit, happy and tired, drinking Chianti before the doors of their houses, and gossip good-humouredly to friends after the day's work. They don't want anything more than that. Poor people all over the world don't want very much; it is not they who make the trouble. And they have always been the same. When we saw them that summer evening long ago in Verona, David quoted some poetry about poor people enjoying themselves at their supper after their labour. I think it was Lucretius, but I can only remember one line, and I am not sure of that:

Non magnis opibus iucunde corpora curant.

4

Soldiers are here at last. A lot of them arrived at Carrick Bay this week. The girls and I were walking along the cliff path when we heard a chorus of jovial whoops. Just above us was a very ugly little hotel from every window of which soldiers' heads were sticking; they were packed so tight that it looked as if the stunted little building must be all solid soldier inside, like a tin of sardines.

I suppose I must look less matronly and more glamorous when viewed from above than I do on the level; or perhaps they were starving for female companionship. Anyway I got a rousing welcome and many compliments on my personal appearance. The girls were much impressed and exclaimed:

'O Mother! Those soldiers are shouting to you. They asked if Sunday is your day off. Do they know you?'

Today we got our share at Porthmerryn. A lot of them are billeted at the hotel where we have lunch. They spent the afternoon drilling on the sands, somewhat hampered by hundreds of admiring babies who sat in rings round their feet. Slightly older children drilled in solemn rows behind them, copying all their movements with great exactitude.

They look quite different from soldiers in the last war. T and all those pink-faced boys in the last war were much more 'military' and more spick and span. These hardly look like soldiers at all. They are armed citizens, dressed shabbily but conveniently for their job. They go about their work with a grim efficiency, and they give the impression of spirits which are neither high nor low. I realise that I have never before seen soldiers on ground where they expect to have to fight. I have only seen them training, on leave, or on parade, never on a potential battlefield. Their homely, bored faces and their shabby reach-me-downs have a poignancy. The Happy Warrior ought to be more dressed up; he ought to have a red coat and a bearskin, or a golden-plumed helmet like Hector. He ought not to look so like an ordinary man going to work in a bus.

Magnus and Mary were watching some of them putting barbed wire round the reservoir. A lady came up to them with that glare of universal misanthropy in her eyes which often denotes a pacifist. She pointed to the soldiers and said:

'Isn't that a horrible sight?'

They said no, they didn't find it so.

She raised her arms to heaven and said:

'I suppose you *want* to see the whole countryside drenched in blood?'

Magnus pondered for a few seconds, and then said, very mildly:

'Yes.'

As if, on thinking it over, he had decided that he did want to see the countryside drenched in blood.

The lady looked rather frightened and hurried on.

Answer fools according to their folly.

5

Nanny, usually so imperturbable, took it into her head to give me the dickens of a fright today. She came rushing in, her hand over her heart, and gasped out:

'Oh … Mrs Aitken's gardener's been up, and he says *they* are in the town, and we must all stay in our houses, and we mustn't be frightened if we hear firing.'

Well, of course I thought *they* were the Germans. Anybody would.

I went all gooseflesh for a minute and my hair stood up on my head like the fretful porcupine's. Then I went onto the back veranda and began to put on my thick boots with nails in them. I've often wondered what I would do if I heard the Germans had landed. Now I know. As I wrestled with the laces I began to tick off in my mind the other things I must do: hide food and maps, put money inside corsets, look out gas masks, ration books and identity cards, have everyone's knapsacks ready packed, and make everyone put on their thick boots. I was perfectly obsessed with the idea of boots, Freud knows why.

Nanny came and stood watching me, breathing heavily, but faintly pleased to have made her soft employer jump.

'How,' I asked, 'did Mrs Aitken's gardener know?'

'He said the Town Crier is going round.'

I laced a second or two longer and then realised that this sounded a bit odd. Surely, even in Porthmerryn an invasion would not be announced in this *Ye Olde Worlde* way.

Just then we heard a distant handbell and a long howl:

'Oyez! Oyez! Oyez! GAWD ... SAVE ... TH' KING ... AND ALL ... TH' NATION...'

Amen, I thought, as we rushed down to the gate.

The Crier is a seedy old man and he doesn't wear a cocked hat any more. They say his last one blew off into the sea twelve years ago and the borough authorities would not buy him another. So he wears a checked cloth cap which he raises whenever he mentions the King. I couldn't make out a word he said but Nanny began to look slightly disappointed.

'Oh,' she said, 'so it's only Our Boys after all.'

'What does he say?'

'He says they're having manoeuvres in the town this morning and will everybody keep out of Fore Street and Gabriel Street, between eleven and twelve, and we must not be nervous if we hear firing, because it's only Our Boys.'

I sat down and took off my boots. For two pins I'd have thrown them at Nanny's head.

✕

We have pretty well made up our minds not to send the children overseas. The government scheme seems to move slowly and there is a general opinion that the dangers on the high seas in the next few months are going to be greater than the dangers here in quiet rural areas. If the government scheme had developed, placing the children of the poor and the prosperous on the same footing, I think we might have put ours down for it, though I'm not sure. We shall never be sure if we did right till the end of the war, when we shall know just how much they have had to suffer by staying. It is an awfully difficult choice for any parents to make.

There is of course the possibility that we may all have to go hungry before we are through with this. But plenty of fine men and women have gone hungry when they were young. And a fine family life, something lasting and valuable in the home background and the influence of one or both parents, matters very much in the production of fine men and women. You find it is so in the cases of 99 per cent of the people you admire in history and among contemporaries. To break up family life, even in order to save the children from hardship or fear, is a very serious thing. But on the other hand I feel that people who for some good reason couldn't keep their children with them here, or ensure for them a life which, though hard, should be fairly tranquil and orderly, would be right to send them away. And people who do keep their children with them *must* go bail with themselves to remain calm and undismayed, whatever happens.

It is obvious that the government fears the risk of sending the children. Meanwhile there is much bitterness because a Cabinet Minister is said to have sent his child over in an American liner which came to collect American citizens. This makes nine out of every ten women foam at the mouth because they think he used his position to pull strings and avoid the danger of sending his child in a British ship. Of course the report may be untrue, but it goes to show how dangerous it would be if there was much of that sort of thing, or even rumours of that sort of thing. The fact that the young Princesses have stayed here seems to reassure a lot of people, who argue that 'the Queen can't think it is going to be so bad'.

I got a batch of letters from abroad today. Everybody seems to think we are licked. I shall have to write these friends and explain that this little old island has to be killed before it can be cooked. It will be easy to say that in letters to Americans, but when I write to Spain I shall have to try to suggest it in a way that will get past the Franquist censorship. They say the Spanish press is only allowed to print pro-Axis news, so I dare say the lady who wrote to me from Seville doesn't realise we have an RAF.

A story has been going round lately about a Spanish censor ringing up headquarters to get instructions:

'Allo Rome?'

'Ja?'

✻

My letters from the USA have been three weeks on the way and are the first I've had from there since France collapsed. Our American friends are terribly worried about our personal fate, but I detect in what they write a kind of exasperated undercurrent, an inner conflict which I know well because we felt it ourselves so much in the pre-war years. Like all normal, decent human beings, they feel their hackles rising at the sight of a bragging bully trying to dominate the world. But reason tells them that men and nations cannot be governed by the impulse that makes them want to kick a bully in the pants.

Ever since 1934 we have had people who told us Germany was becoming a menace and that we ought to fight a preventive war, and I dare say that there are now Americans who want their own country to fight a preventive war. But it is very difficult to get a civilised and democratic people into a preventive war. That's where the dictators have an advantage.

A friend of mine in Kansas says we have not been fighting hard enough because we are not really a democracy. The next few months may make her change her mind about our capacity for fighting but I doubt if she will ever change it about democracy.

Well, by their standards we are not a democracy. There is this class business which they can't stomach. Of course they have snobbery over there; wherever there are human beings you get snobbery of one sort or another; it is an endemic vice. But the traditional, institutional, bred-in-the-bone, dyed-in-the-wool British class distinctions stick in the American gizzard.

What Americans don't realise is that many people here also dislike these things. Another thing they don't realise is how much we are changing. Probably the reason they don't realise it is that the changes are coming from the bottom up, and as they mostly meet our top dogs they don't know much about the bottom. Time and again I've told my friend in Kansas that she doesn't know anything about the real pith and sap and strength and character of the British people. She merely replies:

'If your "ungentry" are all you say they are, why do they let a parcel of adenoidy, dowdy survivals put it over them?'

I tell her there's no use in flogging dead horses. Our people just laugh, like the soldiers in the train.

And then the word 'democracy' does mean something different to Americans from what it does to us. We use it to mean representative government, a constitutional opposition, Habeas Corpus, Magna Carta, trial by jury, the Bill of Rights, freedom of the press, of speech, of religion, free and public justice, and all that. We call those things 'our Liberties' and we will fight like tigers for them.

But Americans, from what I can make out, mean something different, something more mystical and idealistic. I don't quite understand what it is, but it's all mixed up with their conception of Liberty as an almost sacramental possession, not 'our Liberties,' but LIBERTY – something they think they have more of than anybody else, a kind of essence they breathe. And it comprises, too, those virtues which can only flourish in the air of liberty, the full growth and dignity and worth of the human individual.

The explanation, I suppose, lies deep in history. On our side we think of liberty as something which, in theory, we have always had. Our whole progress has been to define it, extend its effectiveness, secure it, build constitutional walls round it which will enable us better to cultivate it. On their side they think of it as something whole and indivisible which was won at one stroke, and which dwells in their Constitution. Their first conception of it springs from the Pilgrim Fathers who sought it that they might better serve God. People escaping from tyrannical slavery in Europe received it like a sacrament the moment they received American citizenship.

I find myself pondering about the USA, more than anything else, almost. I suppose because, if we go down, the world's future, and all that we have cared for and fought for, will lie in their hands. Whether they like it or not they will be the sole trustees for the spirit of mankind.

And, if we don't go down, the only real hope is in a better understanding between the British Empire and the USA. All this would never have happened if we had understood one another better and got on better in the past. This evil has grown up only because the two great powers that might have checked it were antagonistic and suspicious of one another. I think often of Low's cartoon showing Britannia and Columbia sitting at either end of a see-saw, glaring at each other, while Japan sits gaily on the top and says:

'Very nice? Yes? As long as Honourable Ladies continue to sit apart.'

6

We have just had our first air-raid alarm. It has given poor little Porthmerryn quite a jolt.

I was in Fore Street when the sirens went and their dying howl was merged into a sinister roar as three German planes came over from the south. Fore Street was crowded with shoppers, holiday folk in beach suits eating ices, children, perambulators, bicycles, and old ladies with shopping baskets. We all stood stupidly gazing upwards. Suddenly a man came charging down the hill. Nobody knows who he was. His face was a dirty yellow-white and he kept shouting:

'Here they are! Here come the bombs! Look out for yourselves! Run! Run! Here they come! Bombs!'

I never saw a grown man mad with fear before. It was shocking … awful. Some say he was Fifth Column, but I think he was just yellow. He started a pretty little panic. People began to run about distractedly. There was no cover. All the shops slammed and locked their doors when the sirens went, and there are no shelters in Porthmerryn, though I bet there will be after this. People charged up and down the hill, dragging shrieking children behind them, tangling with perambulators and pushing old people into the road. If there had been bombs Fore Street would have been a nice mess.

I got involved with an arthritic old lady who had been pushed down. We turned into a side street where we found an open doorway and took shelter. A nice smell of new bread was wafted at us up some stone steps, so we went down a little way and found ourselves in a great underground bakery. Three bakers in white coats were busy at the ovens and boys were going to and fro with wire trays of buns and splits and pasties. They welcomed us kindly and let us sit on the steps. I said there was a raid on and the oldest baker, quite an old man, said:

'Iss fay, m'dear, so 'tes I b'lieve.'

I was enchanted to be thus addressed in the ancient dialect of the region. I had thought that nobody ever says 'Iss fay' outside a novel.

We sat there for a bit. I was still feeling sick at the memory of that awful man screaming. My old lady started telling me about earthquakes, which she seemed to be quite accustomed to, having lived in some part of the world, I forget where, which has them most days. She said she wouldn't think anything of air raids after earthquakes if only it hadn't been for her rheumatism. She said in an air raid you are in the hands of man, and there is some limit to what he can do. But in an earthquake you are in the hands of God and there is no knowing. She said she had borne three children during earthquakes, and in one place where she was an earthquake used to happen every morning at eleven, just when she was sitting at her desk doing accounts, and the desk used to jump and hit her face every morning at eleven sharp. She didn't look like a liar either.

After a while I said I didn't think it could really be a raid as we had heard no bombs. She said mysteriously:

'My dear, they say you never *do* hear the bomb that kills you.'

As if we might both be dead and not know it.

The bakers gave us each a lovely pasty fresh from the oven.

I was worried about the children and at last I decided to go home and not wait for the 'All Clear'. We had heard no more planes after that first lot. So I said good-bye to the old lady and the bakers and ventured forth.

Fore Street was quite empty. Where all the people had got to I don't know. There was nobody to be seen but a warden in a tin hat who immediately told me to take cover because there was an air raid. I asked if everybody is supposed to leave off whatever they are doing and get under cover whenever the sirens go. He said yes, but I can't believe it. When the big show starts there will be precious few places in this island where the sirens don't go every day and all day long. If we all stick under cover nobody from Land's End to John o' Groats will be able to so much as post a letter. The whole life of the country will stop. We shall have to modify that idea.

I went on up the hill. Smith's was open, so I went in there to collect our newspapers. A lot of people had taken refuge in the circulating library at the back and were sitting in a semicircle of chairs, like people at a lecture or concert. They were all quite silent and, by some chance, all old. Their stricken, dismayed old faces were very pathetic as they sat there waiting for they knew not what. Really I think this war is worse for old people than for anybody. In these preposterous conditions the most valuable thing to have, after courage, is adaptability – quickness to grasp new ideas and problems, and power to improvise solutions – and old people are not, as a rule, adaptable. They are game enough for anything, but their minds have slowed up and they don't take things in quickly.

When I got home I found that Miss Wright had put all the children under the kitchen table and smothered them in eiderdowns to protect them from glass splinters. The poor things were nearly suffocated, for it was a hot day. But I don't think that is necessary. If a bomb hits this house we shall all go straight to heaven, for it's as fragile as a matchbox. But it's a million to one a bomb won't hit this house. If any are dropped on Porthmerryn they will be aimed at the harbour, not up here. If we get one it will be a mistake, and the Germans are supposed to be very systematic and not make mistakes.

7

Claire's father is down for the week-end. He looks ghastly, but he has more than the war to worry him, for Claire's mother is very ill again. She has had one major operation, and now she has to have another. He, being a doctor, knows too much. He won't talk about it, but I can see he is tortured with anxiety. Claire was over the moon to see him. I pray that nothing terrible is in store for her. She is so happy with us, and is growing so tall and graceful.

I asked him what people in London are thinking about the war now. He laughed and said there are eight million people in London and he doesn't happen to know what they are all thinking. And I realise how provincial I am getting.

That is the great difference between London and Manchester or Liverpool or Birmingham. Anybody living in those towns could give some account of the general run of opinion among his fellow-citizens. A Londoner couldn't. People there live in their own kraals, spiritually or physically. London does not lead or represent opinion in the country. Stanley Baldwin showed how well he knew this during the abdication hullabaloo. When the MPs couldn't make up their minds he told them all to get down to the provinces, to their constituencies, for the week-end and find out what the country was thinking, which they would never know in London. So they did, and came back on Monday with their minds made up.

※

I went to the pictures with Claire's father, the first jaunt I've had for three months. I've been to the pictures only once since the war started, and I'm sure it's bad for one to be cut off from all those accustomed stimulants.

It was an old picture, the Marx Brothers in *At the Circus*. Pictures don't get down here till they are pretty old, but luckily we had not seen it.

Generally I laugh extravagantly over the Marx Brothers and then feel depressed afterwards, as if my laughter had been exciting but not refreshing. They have always seemed to me like the jesters of the damned, making cracks in a doomed world for people who, like the revellers in Poe's poem, can

Laugh – but smile no more.

They are incomparable comedians but they have no humanism. Chaplin, on the other hand, is soaked in it. He takes human nature as the basis of all his fantasies. As a street scavenger, sweeping up horse-manure, his hopeful glance after a passing elephant is a comment on all human ambition. It has got Austerlitz, and the *Chaconne*, and the Sistine Chapel in it: 'Ah ... what could I not achieve if ...' But the Marx Brothers generally wash out the human element. They rely upon violent disconcertment, incongruity, disassociation of ideas.

In this picture, however, there is a sequence which took us entirely by surprise: Harpo playing to a lot of Negroes. There was one shot which was beautiful: the harp took up most of it, with Harpo's face in one corner, his real face, mad no longer, but for an instant clever, sensitive, and melancholy. And through the harp strings, as if through bars, the face of a little coloured girl, listening.

It was the sort of thing which can only be done in the pictures, this sudden juxtaposition of the Jew and the Negro, and the long sorrow of their races, that look which says:

For I am a stranger with Thee, and a sojourner, as all my fathers were.

8

I have had a letter from our friend Ursula, up in the north, which has taken me by surprise.

She and Stephen, her husband, are the most thorough-paced idealists we know. They are getting quite old now in body, but very, very good people don't age quickly in spirit. Nothing so preserves vitality as innocence and single-mindedness. All their lives they have been striving to do as they would be done by. They are vegetarians because they think it is degrading to require fellow-creatures to be butchers. They don't wear fur or feathers. They buy no sweated goods. They belong to every known society for making the world a better place. They write protesting letters to their MP whenever they think this country is behaving badly – which is very often.

But they differ from most humanitarians in that they are extremely genial and like their fellow-men individually as well as in the mass. They like parties and they are not teetotalers. Their hatred is reserved for abstract beings like the Gestapo and the 'Madams' who figure in the League of Nations report on the White Slave Traffic. They read things like League of Nations Reports and Blue Books all through. I have heard Ursula grow very vindictive about those awful Madams, but I'm sure if she found one on her doorstep looking hot and tired she would offer her a cup of tea and a bunch of violets out of the garden, because that is what she would do to anybody who looked hot and tired.

Now I should have thought that among all our friends Ursula and Stephen would have been the most distraught, heart-broken, and horrified by the events of the summer. But not at all. Ursula writes in the highest spirits. And suddenly I see that it is the idealists, not the materialists, who feel most at home in this tornado of physical destruction. They are in their element. Everybody round them is behaving as they themselves have been behaving all their lives: casting self aside, ready to sacrifice all for a great cause. An idealist, in normal times, is a bit lonely and puzzled. The behaviour of his neighbours saddens him if he is amiable and maddens him if he is not. But in times of great ordeal and heroism he has the delightfully novel sensation of coming on with the crowd. For a while, at least, everybody agrees with his view of life.

Idealists are valuable in war time, but when peace comes they are a danger, and generally, in the end, they are badly disillusioned. It is the trimmers who make peace treaties, and there is an unbridgeable gulf between idealists and trimmers. That must be so. Men can't live for ever at the idealist's pitch. A nation can be purely noble for a short period, and during that period can achieve some great advance towards an ideal, can secure some great new principle of freedom and justice. But it is in the long run the trimmers, the really great trimmers, who combine artfulness with principle, who decide how far that advance can go. *Paris vaut une Messe* shocks an idealist but it expressed the will of France.

Great trimmers are not without ideals, but they concentrate on what they can secure and lose little sleep on what they are obliged to throw overboard. They have strong but not tender consciences. No great cause was ever secured without them. They understand the average sensual man, the *mean*, as the idealist does not, and can guess more exactly the degree of courage and self-sacrifice he is likely to bring to the support of an idea. And they can tell what he is likely to desire when he awakens from his dream of heroism – what, later, he will think he fought for. If that is not secured he will feel frustrated and disillusioned. I have always felt that the reason it wasn't secured in 1919 was that there were no top-notch trimmers at Versailles.

President Wilson, for instance, was anything but a trimmer. He was an idealist. He set up for his country, when it went into the first World War, the noble, crusading ideal of 'making the world safe for Democracy'. But some American friends of mine who give a great deal of thought to international affairs say that was not the fundamental thing for which the United States fought. They say it fought for the simple reason that its sovereignty as a nation was threatened. Germany was torpedoing its ships, intriguing against it in Mexico, and promoting disorder and sabotage within its borders. The United States, they tell me, went to war to stop these things. And it did stop them. But the Wilsonian phrase stuck, and as the world was not made safe for Democracy, frustration, disillusionment and cynicism resulted.

※

Thinking of the problems of another European peace, I wonder if we have any great trimmers to see us through. Who are they? Winston? Roosevelt? Or somebody who hasn't come up yet? Funny if it turned out to be an Italian or a German. Roosevelt sounds to me like a very good trimmer. But whoever does the job, Ursula and Stephen will be bitterly disappointed with the outcome.

※

The children and I went for a walk along the coast today. We came to a headland about five miles from Porthmerryn, a wild, lonely place, overlooking a little cove, where a steep path leads up from a hidden beach. We wondered what would stop the Jerries landing here some dark night. Nobody seemed to be on the lookout. Then, when we were scrambling over a heap of rocks and furze bushes, we saw a human eye observing us from a crack. It wasn't a natural heap, but a cunningly concealed fort, and it was full of soldiers. We said:

'Oh! So this cove is guarded after all.'
A cockney voice from inside the furze bushes said:
'We're not ser green as we're cabbage-looking.'

Chapter Five

August: 'Owed by So Many to So Few'

1

We are getting quite used to the sirens. Nobody runs about Fore Street any more when they go. And, as I expected, nobody leaves off what they are doing and takes cover, unless there are planes coming right over. But I notice that when the alert goes everyone pauses for half a second and then moves rather more briskly. They don't saunter during an alert.

I am happy because David is with us for a whole fortnight. I couldn't have believed in June that I should be as light-hearted as this in August, with the battle over our heads growing fiercer every day, and the invasion still in front of us. David said the other day that I don't look much like Suffering Britain. At which Ellen remarked:

'A woman, Mr Seagrave, is all love.'

Which is a quotation from *Masterman Ready*, a favourite book of theirs, about an early Victorian family wrecked on a desert island. When Mr Seagrave remarked to the old salt, Ready, how strange it was that Mrs Seagrave, a delicate, a refined woman, should settle down so contentedly to life on a coral reef, Ready said:

'A woman is all love, and if she has but her husband and children with her, and in good health, she will make herself happy almost anywhere.'

There is a lot of truth in it.

It is the holidays. Miss Wright has twitched her mantle blue and gone off to teach another family of children up in the north. I shan't ever forget her tough expression when she said that Hitler couldn't make Nazis of us, the day Belgium went out. I asked David if he remembered it, and he said indeed he does. He says he often thinks of it, and thanks God that we have such a lot of Miss Wrights in this country.

We are taking the children out every day to picnics in old haunts where Viola and I used to picnic when we were girls. Yesterday we went to a sweet valley where very few people ever go. It is a long walk, miles from anywhere, and not easy to find. Gentle hills, richly wooded with fine old oaks and beeches, slope down to the river. They are the best woods I know for primroses. There is a flat floor between the hills, about a quarter of a mile wide, partly reed and osier beds, partly very green grass, where the river winds and curves among the willows and bulrushes. You see kingfishers there. The water is a bright blue-green, since it springs from limestone hills, and in places there are patches of red weed which give it a rainbow look. It is very clear. I have seen no water that colour except the Sorgues, running down from Vaucluse to the Rhône; that river is the same bright colour.

The stream is quite shallow, not more than four feet deep anywhere, and it runs swiftly, almost level with the grassy meadow. The current is so strong that nobody could swim against it. The proper way to bathe there is to go up as far as you can, to where the reed beds begin, and swim or float downstream. In some places it goes down a little slope and you get washed over the red weeds with a long 'swish' which we call shooting the rapids. I like best to go down floating on my back, just letting the current take me all the way, watching the kingfishers, and the tapestried foliage on the hillside, and the quiet sky, which always seems to be very low over the valley.

When you get down to the lower reed beds you come out and run over the soft warm grass back to the beginning again. Viola and I used to spend whole days doing this over and over again. I have often thought of it on hot days in London and wondered if it seemed so perfect because we were young then, and if now it would be just a place like any other. But it is still the place. I am glad I have had one bathe there with David and the children before … before whatever is to come, comes.

I never saw it lovelier than yesterday. I was full of 'this demi-Paradise, this other Eden' sentiments, and when I was sure nobody was looking I knelt down and kissed the grass. I suppose no German would have to hide before he saluted his fatherland. Who hides behind yon briary bush? An Englishman, quoting Richard II to himself, and kissing his native soil.

2

David and I put on our tidy clothes and our most staid expressions and went to inspect the school to which we mean to send the three girls in the autumn. It has evacuated itself here lately from the East Coast and will take day pupils. The teaching seems to be admirable, far superior to that of any of the other schools within reach, and I have looked at them all.

But I'm not quite happy about it. It's all a little too exclusive. I have seen the boarders in church – pretty, well-groomed little creatures, with bright hair and clear complexions. Their tonsils have been removed and their crooked teeth straightened by the best men in Harley Street, I am sure. Golf, riding and ballroom dancing are included in the list of extra subjects. The well-trained parlour-maid who opened the door to us said that the headmistress was out in the garden with 'the young ladies', for some of the girls are spending the holidays here.

Young ladies. Well …

Don't I want our girls to grow up young ladies? Yes, I do. But rather a new sort of lady. And I fear this is a nursery for the more old-fashioned bloom.

Perhaps it is quite enough simply to say that I want them to have good manners. But no person can have the best kind of manners unless he is absolutely sure of his own social position, so sure of it that he never worries about it or thinks of it, is never uneasy in any company, is never aggressive or obsequious, haughty or servile, flustered, arrogant, or ostentatious. A code of manners can be imposed and followed, but it is not the genuine thing, it won't stand any real test, unless it springs from some inner sense of worth. All virtues in human intercourse must spring from that: simplicity, dignity, delicacy, consideration for others, the power to disagree without becoming offensive, and to be disagreed with without taking offence. And all the accomplishments too – the composure and urbanity and graciousness of people – who have a social gift. Without that inward sense of worth, polished manners mean just nothing. They are a parlour trick for savages.

I can't bring the children up as I was brought up. My mother had good manners. But she was securely entrenched in a class creed which I have rejected. Why, she once even went so far as to tell us we needn't worry over the meaning of the Seventh Commandment 'because people in our class never break it.'

When I grew older I ventured to chaff her about this. But she stuck to her guns, and said:

'No, I really think a woman who could commit adultery couldn't be quite a lady.'

I want the children to have that sense of worth and dignity; but it must not be founded on class. It must spring from something different, something I can believe in, something which all children can eventually share.

Perhaps that thing is being brought to birth now, in this year of travail. If we get through this we may come out of it in a real and profound sense a nation of aristocrats, a nation with more inner pride at having lived through the Battle of Britain, having shared in the struggle, than any one class in this country has ever felt before.

I have kept the children in England, and sometimes in moments of despondency and timidity I am sorry I did. I wish they were away in safety, overseas. And then at other times I feel that it is very important that they should take part in this experience which the huge majority of children here are going through; that enormous changes are taking place which we don't quite grasp yet. By the grace of God we may emerge from this ordeal a more admirable society than we were when we went in. I want the children to be worthy citizens, not museum-pieces kept in cold storage. Physically they run risks. Spiritually it is probably an advantage that they should not be cut off from the bulk of their contemporaries.

I heard the other day from a friend who went to America at the end of May with her children. Her letter sounded very moany and groany. She was still back in May, while we, over here, have got on to August. I felt as if she was out of touch with us. It made me glad we hadn't gone.

So I don't quite like this school which strikes me as belonging too much to the past. But it will have to do for the present, as the level of scholarship in the others is very poor.

And I liked the headmistress, when she appeared. She was at my College at Oxford. She brightened when I said that all three girls were to have professions and would, I hope, go to college. She is a well-educated woman, which is more than most schoolma'ams are, and does not regard all parents as illiterate Yahoos. When I get to know her better I shall try to discover her slant on this young lady problem. She has her living to earn and has to deliver the goods that are in demand, but I'd like to know what goods she would prefer to deliver if she had her choice.

David doesn't worry about these things so much. He

enquired about the school air-raid shelter. He would like his daughters to be worthy citizens, but he is more concerned about bombs, and what will happen to them and their dam in the next few months. But he did ask if Ellen could learn Greek. And when we came away he lamented that she is not a boy, because, said he, such brains are wasted on a woman.

I blew up with a wealth of dynamic vituperation which was almost pre-war.

3

Today we picnicked at a wild, rocky cove with a wonderful natural swimming pool at low tide.

Suddenly David said:

'This is August 15, the day Hitler said he would dictate a world peace from Buck House.'

After luncheon I climbed along the cliffs to Spaniard's Point and sat on the end of it and contemplated the sea. Suddenly a huge plane shot down out of the sky. I don't know where it came from, but as it roared over Spaniard's Point I could see the black crosses on it.

I wasn't frightened, I was in such a rage. My skin crawled on my bones and I jumped up and shouted:

'You …!' (A word no lady would use.)

And I picked up a small stone and flung it at the plane. At least I meant to fling it at the plane, but it went in the opposite direction, as things always do when I throw them.

Now I understand how it was that T, the mildest and most good-tempered of boys, was able to lead a bayonet charge. I never could quite believe it before. But I'd have bayoneted those Huns with pleasure if I had had the chance.

Nor do I feel in the least ashamed of myself for giving way to warlike passions. They are not quite the same as revengeful passions.

I am sure that the pacifists are wrong and that God gave us our combative instincts, just as he gave all our other instincts, to be used, not disowned. They are part of a man and I do not believe that we ought to unman ourselves. Morality lies in learning how and when to use them. And it is just quibble to say that Our Lord's action was only 'symbolic' when he flew into a rage and drove the money changers out of the temple. Symbolic of what? He was chasing them off his premises in a very violent manner and they were really scared. Pacifists say he didn't hit them very hard, but the Book doesn't say so any more than it says that the wine at Cana of Galilee was non-alcoholic.

In the blueprint of *homo sapiens*, laid up in heaven, there is an emergency power house called rage and we were meant to rely upon it in certain circumstances.

I wonder if that bomber was looking for Buck House.

When we got home we heard, on the nine o'clock news, that the RAF have shot down 160 of their planes today. A tremendous air battle has been raging all over the country.

4

A study in manners.

I met Mrs Harkness with Duncan, her five-year-old evacué. When she stopped to speak to me he gave me a beaming smile and snatched off his linen sun hat. He was carrying her shopping basket for her. She tells me he always does, taking it firmly from her and saying:

'I'll carry that for yer.'

He is used to carrying things for his Mum. And when the children came down here Mum seems to have told them to help the lady in all the little ways they could, as if they were at home.

Ten minutes later I met Mrs Allsop, of Upalong, with her six-year-old grandson, Michael, who has a day nursery and a night nursery and a college-trained nurse. He also had a hat, which he did not take off, but after some coaxing he was induced to offer me his left hand to shake. His grandmother carried his spade and bucket for him.

Mrs Allsop asked if we were bathing this afternoon, as Michael's nurse is off and he has nobody to bathe with. I said we were all bathing, and the Harkness Vackies too, and he was welcome to join us. Mrs Allsop looked doubtful.

'I don't think his mother would care for him to mix with the Vackies. One doesn't want him to pick up rough ways.'

I said indignantly that the Harkness children would not be likely to teach rough ways to anybody. Their manners are perfect.

'Oh, yes, my dear. But what about the accent?'

Michael spends most of his time with his nurse, and her accent would frighten the French – it is a most unpleasant example of the mincing, 'refaned' mumble. I've no doubt but that she looks down on our Nanny for her soft, characteristic Berkshire, with its homely proverbs and country idioms.

The accent of the Harkness Vackies, by the way, is undergoing a sea change. They have picked up a strong local inflection from their Downalong schoolfellows, and they have acquired a certain gentleness of utterance from Lily Harkness herself. She told me that lately they talked on the telephone to their father, and their comment was:

'Coo! Don't 'e talk Cockney!'

5

We do seem to be winning this phase of the war in the air. Our infants up there are doing wonders. They shoot down quantities of bombers and fighters. The attempt to clear the

RAF out of the air and smash our aerodromes has failed.

We expect the next phase to be the bombing of the big towns and the attempt to smash industry. The preparations for shelters and such matters seem, as far as we can make out, to be exactly what they were in June.

Everybody loves the RAF. Today I saw a young pilot walking down Fore Street – one of those pink, stodgy-looking boys who are working these miracles, and are sometimes brought to the microphone and made to tell us about it in short, stodgy sentences. People turned to look after him, as they passed, with a kind of worship in their eyes. The shop people came to their doors, and all the way up the hill people turned round to stare. We did not cheer. There was a feeling in the air which went far beyond cheering.

For there is only such a handful of them compared with the *Luftwaffe*, and they have so few machines. But that handful stands in the pass, and all our hopes, the hopes of free men all over the world, hang on them. If they failed us night would fall.

✕

A lot more Gluebottoms have arrived, bringing with them a crop of bomb stories. Two particularly revolting females have come to our luncheon hotel – hefty wenches who ought to be helping with the harvest. They said they had come from Brighton and that Brighton railway station is completely demolished. Poor Nanny, whose sister has a little shop right by Brighton station, was dreadfully upset till she got a letter from her sister written after these sluts came here, saying that there have been no bombs on Brighton at all.

This week we had a lovely rumour. Our soldiers were practising machine-gunning, shooting at a buoy out in the harbour. Next day it was reported in a neighbouring village that a boy had been hit by machine-guns on our beach.

Next day it was said in Penmorvah that German planes had machine-gunned our beach and killed sixty children. Buoy – boy – children. That's how rumours start.

6

David has gone, and I am feeling most unlike Mrs Seagrave. I am sure that London will be horribly bombed before I see him again at the end of September. But then I have been sure of that every time I have said good-bye to him since September, 1939. But *this* time it will happen.

✕

Charles said today:

'It's so sad. In war time we can never see *my grandmother's parlour.*'

He meant that phantom room you see outside the window in the dusk, when the lamps are lighted and the curtains not drawn – chairs and tables with the garden bushes showing through them. The blackout has banished it. I had forgotten it, and the fascination it has for all children. But I am glad darling Charles remembers.

✕

My little friend Bob, who is training for the RAF, is here on leave. I have not seen him since he grew up, but he is not much changed since the days when I made balliechutes for him and taught him to swim. He has the same yellow head and the same look of T. (Good God! T would have been forty-two now, if he had lived.)

Bob is a sweetie pie but I can't talk to him because he belongs to the younger generation, and I am all at sea with his section of the YG. We have different Bibles. Mine is Mill *On Liberty*, and theirs is *Das Kapital*. I sometimes comfort myself by reflecting that I have read mine all through and nobody has read theirs. But it seems that we have no meeting ground. We are full of goodwill towards one another, but a conversation between us is like that scene in the original version of *The Cherry Orchard* between the governess and the old butler, and he talks Russian and she talks German and neither has the faintest idea of what the other is saying.

✕

Bob: Of course Russia doesn't want Britain to win. It would mean the victory of moderation and compromise and common sense and all that.

Me: You think those are bad things?

Bob: Oh, yes. They would delay the Revolution.

Me: Have we got to have a revolution?

Bob: Oh, yes. Nobody here wants Communism. I used to think the workers could be educated up to it, but it's no use. They don't want it.

Me: Why do we have to have it if nobody wants it?

Bob: Because Communism is right.

Me: I'll accept any social changes but I won't give up democracy.

Bob: Democracy is proved to be a failure.

Me: Is Communism proved to be a success? I

Bob: Oh, yes. In Russia.

Me: How do you know? After twenty-three years they hardly dare let their sympathisers go there. They daren't let any of their own people travel or see what conditions are in other countries. If it was such a success wouldn't they be asking the world to come and look?

✕

But you can't argue with a Totalitarian, because they don't believe in argument. They don't argue much even among themselves. They have purges. I once heard a lot of Communists arguing at a sherry party, and thought that now they had actually begun to disagree I might learn something. But in five minutes I crawled under the table to get out of the scrap and lay there listening to the crunch of horn-rimmed spectacles.

I said to Bob, quoting Voltaire,

'I disapprove of what you say, but I will defend to the death your right to say it.'

He blinked. All that is implied by that quotation means just nothing to him.

If T had lived he would now be in the prime of life. He and his contemporaries, killed in the last war, are a great loss to these young men in the twenties. They would have made some kind of link between the old world and the new. The country has been run by old men, and this is one of the consequences, both here and in France. There have not been enough forty-year-old leaders of thought, because so many were cut off. There has been a violent revolt in ideas rather than a natural development. Never in history has youth been left so stranded.

Some Communists want Hitler to win, because they think that will bring about the Revolution. But Bob, I gather, takes a more hopeful view. He thinks we might have the Revolution now, purge Winston, and set up a Soviet, and then we would win the war. The Germans, he said, would be so much reassured that they would immediately sack Hitler, and Russia would come in on our side. I said that the Finnish campaign didn't encourage one to think that Russia would be an efficient ally. He said that Stalin never fought very hard in the Finnish campaign because he was so sorry for the poor Finns.

※

We still go on winning the air battle. It is said that not a single bomber returned to Germany of all those which set out to attack Croydon aerodrome.

Claire's father says the hospital porter borrowed his binoculars to lend to his old mother, who lives down at Croydon. She likes to sit on her roof and have a good look at all the houses which have been knocked down. The porter says it cheers her up no end.

7

Viola and her children are at a village some fifty miles up the coast. This week we all went over to see them. Nanny, Lucy, and Charles went only for the day, but Ellen and I stayed there for a couple of nights.

I thought it would do Ellen good to get a little change. She has grown and matured a lot these last months and gets very bored with Claire and Lucy, who, since they have no ponies, have got a craze for playing marbles. They each have a racing stud of marbles, and they talk of nothing else. Ellen complained to me:

'It was bad enough when they spent the whole day playing *with* marbles. But now they have sunk to a lower depth of imbecility and have begun to pretend that they are marbles themselves.'

So I thought she had better play for a while with Viola's Dinah, who is a very different type of child.

We hired a car to go over. It's strange that one can still get petrol for a jaunt of a hundred miles, but so it is. I only hope it means our petrol supplies are inexhaustible and not that somebody in Whitehall has gone fishing.

It was a most interesting drive, though the absence of signposts was a bore, as we could never quite tell where we were. We saw balloon barrages in the distance, round several towns which did not have any three months ago. There are barriers across the roads every little way, and they are mostly very well camouflaged. Behind each barrier stands a battered old car, which we suppose is to be driven into the gap if the barrier is closed suddenly. They look pretty flimsy to me. I'd have thought a tank could drive straight through them. But our driver told us mysteriously that there was more in them than you would think. Perhaps they are arranged to explode if touched.

There are forts and blockhouses at all crossroads, and every village has a fort at either end of it. I really think if the Germans came to these parts they would find it hard to move across the country. The fields are all small and fenced by high stone walls, which would impede cross-country movements. It would be very different from sweeping along the poplar-edged roads and unfenced fields of the Low Countries and northern France, where there is not so much natural cover for defending forces. Here at every turn are copses, spinneys, and thorny brakes which can conceal gun posts. And they say the preparations down here are nothing like what has been done farther east, partly I suppose because this is naturally an easy territory to defend.

A man was talking on the wireless the other day about our defences, and he said if the Germans come it won't be a case of breaking through a line, or of defence in depth, because our defensive zone is from one sea to the other. They would encounter the same preparations and the same resistance wherever they went: we are all a Maginot Line, not an undefended country with a wall round it, as France was. If they come, we are to stay put. This may be rather a hard order to carry out, as I expect they will try to terrorise the people in any place they get to, and do atrocities in the hope of starting panic. But we must stick it. And I hope they won't get much time for such things.

✳

Viola and her family are in fine health and spirits. She had written to me that the little cove where they are staying is 'utterly quiet and peaceful'. So I was somewhat surprised to discover that they have been raided every night for a fortnight, and have had far more larks than we ever had at Porthmerryn. There is an objective only two miles away, and the Jerries are determined to get it, according to the other inmates of Viola's boarding house. But she says, quite firmly, that there have been *no* raids.

Everyone has his own way of bearing a war. Mine is to speculate on what will happen afterwards, which rather annoys David. Viola's is to say there is no war, or rather that she doesn't have to notice the war. She is a very strong-minded woman and has always been able to ignore anything which does not suit her. It would be inconvenient for her to move just now; they have booked their rooms here and her house is shut up. I imagine there has been some little dispute between her and her husband, who has lately been down here on leave and was probably alarmed to find the place so lively and urged her to take the children away. But she rejects any suggestion that the place is dangerous with a kind of icy fury which I know well from old times. She has been like that from the cradle and will be to the grave.

We had a lovely day, bathing and exploring smugglers' caves. The sea is several degrees warmer than it is at Porthmerryn, I don't know why. The great excitement is a magnetic mine which drifted in one day and was made harmless by the coastguards, and now rolls about the bay, washed into a different place every day. At low tide it lies on the sands and all the infant population take turns to climb up it and jump off it. Dinah and Terence, Viola's two elder children, greeted us before our car had even stopped with shouts of:

'We've got a magnetic mine. Have you got a magnetic mine? Bet you haven't got a magnetic mine at your old Porthmerryn.'

Nanny, Lucy, and Charles set off home after tea, promising to get out of the car immediately and go into the nearest house if they should run into a raid on the way. I am rather nervous about stories of cars being machine-gunned. Viola listened to all my fussy instructions impatiently and remarked she wondered I hadn't hired a tank to take them home.

✕

The people in the boarding house were a very nice crowd, mostly mothers with children, and nobody of the Gluebottom type. They have a custom of all going up to the village in a bunch after supper to hear the news at a little café, for the boarding house coffee is vile and the place has no wireless. It was a delicious warm evening and we sat in the garden under a mulberry tree and sipped coffee and smelt the night stocks. I enjoyed the change of scene and company very much. Our conversation was what David would call Gorgo and Praxinoe. We repeated ourselves a great deal, were inconsequent and trivial, and were slightly inclined to laugh at men. David cannot believe that I enjoy that kind of chatter and thinks I do it just to be matey. But I like women and I like gossiping with women. It's very restful.

In the party there was a charming little person with a face like a kitten and very pretty curls. She is the kind of woman I would marry if I were a man. Her voice was soft and rather plaintive, but pleasing; her look, her air, full of grace and charm and good humour. She was one of those women who are like a nosegay of flowers in a room. I don't think she can have been under forty, she gave an impression of maturity and experience, but at the same time had an innocence, a naive, almost childish, freshness, which was quite delightful. I don't suppose she is a bit clever, but she succeeds at the job of being a woman.

Her two tall schoolboy sons had volunteered to help the

Home Guard during their holidays. When they had had their coffee they went off for a spell of duty. That kind of a woman nearly always has sons. It was pleasant to see her tie their mufflers round their necks and sigh:

'Now go and guard us. You'll find a thermos flask of soup in your room when you come in.'

Just as the news bulletin finished we heard a whistle. The village is too small to have a siren, so the local warden, who keeps the general shop, gives the warnings on a whistle. If he has on a tin hat it means 'Alert', and if he has a cap it 'means 'All Clear'. When the whistle goes everyone rushes out to look at him and see which it is.

We thought we had better get home, as we had most of us left children unattended at the boarding house. But Viola said there was no hurry, at which everybody smiled. I expect her refusal to have traffic with the war is a bit of a joke among them. We started down the lane and heard the zoomzazoomzazoomzazoomza of a German bomber. (I don't care what anybody says: it has got a different noise from our planes, which go zoomzoomzoom.) Searchlights pencilled the sky, AA guns began firing from the surrounding hills, and shells burst overhead. There was a sudden flare of incendiaries in the direction of the Objective, and a crump which sounded like heavy explosive. According to the others the nightly entertainment had started an hour before its usual time.

We ought by rights to have taken cover or lain down flat under a hedge. But we were worried about our children and hurried on as best we could. We could not run, as we were crossing a field full of rabbit holes and it was getting dark. Viola simply sauntered and told us about a Mozart record she had just bought. The rest of us scuttled on in silence until little Kittenface murmured plaintively:

'Me no likee!'

Which was so exactly what we were all feeling it that we burst out laughing.

We found all the children hanging excitedly out of the boarding-house windows watching the raid. I began fussing and said they should keep away from the windows. Viola had just begun a crushing:

'My dear Margaret. It's quite unnecessary ...' when there came a loud CRUMP a good deal nearer than previous crumps and she hastily seized Dinah and thrust her under the nearest bed.

After that the raid seemed to die down for a while and we all went to bed. Viola and I were sleeping together, a thing we haven't done in the years since we both married.

She was irritated because she had given herself away and put Dinah under the bed, and I caught it on all sides. She said what a pity it is that I have got so thin, and my hair so grey; I am too young to have grey hair, but that's what comes of fussing. And why have I given up my fringe? Curls don't suit me at all. And what shall I do if Ellen's feet grow any larger?

Also we fought as to who should get out of bed to turn out the light. She said I had to because her husband always did. I said:

'Poor man.'

Altogether it was quite like old times. The cares and sorrows of years slipped away and I almost expected to hear Mother knocking on the wall to tell us girls to stop talking and go to sleep.

After we had lain in the darkness for some time she asked suspiciously:

'Is that noise you eating something?'

I said I was. Chocolate. And gave her some. There was silence for some time, broken only by sounds of munching. Then some bangs. She said sleepily:

'Darling ... this is perfectly delicious chocolate. Got any more?'

Bang! Bang! CRRRRUMP!

I said:

'You shall have some more if you'll tell me what that was.'

A long pause. Then she murmured:

'A bum ...'

So she got some more chocolate.

✕

The whistle kept blowing all night, sometimes waking us up, sometimes not, so we quite lost count. As Kittenface said next morning, they might just as well blow it at blackout-time and say: That's you for the night.

I was finally wakened to meet the horrified eyes of Viola's baby, who had toddled in to say good morning to her and found my tousled curls on the pillow where he was accustomed to see his father's neat, grizzled pate. He gave me one deeply disapproving glance and then trotted out as if he would be no party to such goings on.

We had a bathe in the morning. We had no sooner got into the sea than that everlasting whistle went and a zoomzazoom came along. We all dashed for the caves where we had left our clothes, except Viola, who took her baby for a walk on an exposed bit of the cliff and told him, I dare say, to look at the pretty Heinkels. The caves made a good shelter but a number of soldiers suddenly appeared and warned us not to come out lest we should be machine-gunned – much to the embarrassment of various modest old ladies who were trying to dress. We heard in the cave next to ours: 'Go away, young man! Go away at once!'

In the afternoon we took our tea up to the lighthouse. Here we had a fine view of all the surrounding country. We saw a great many smouldering fires, doubtless from the incendiaries of the night before. One must, I think, have hit a petrol dump. I never saw such a column of smoke, so high, so dense, or so black. It went up hundreds of feet and the people say they saw it over in Porthmerryn. I pointed it out to Viola and she said it was bracken burning, probably – that they often burn down the bracken on the hillsides this time of year.

I said that bracken smoke is a low, white smudge.

'Not in this district,' she said firmly. 'Here it's always black.'

Incredible woman. But in many ways it is most refreshing to be with her. She has managed to keep so much of her pre-war bounce and gaiety.

We came home the next day. Ellen had enjoyed it tremendously. And she was greatly delighted at having seen a raid at such close quarters.

'But I shan't boast about it to Lucy and Claire,' she said. 'It's so hard on them to have missed it.'

8

My journal seems to be getting much more scrappy. May and June fill up many more pages than July and August. But I am too busy to write it in the day, and at night I sleep instead of sitting up writing. Besides, everything seems to have got set and hardened these last two months. In May and June 'the whole world was in a state of chassis', to quote the Paycock. Everything was slipping and sliding and changing, and one never knew what was going to happen, or what to think, and the lifebelt of today became the straw of tomorrow. I felt bound to slap every day's impressions and reflections down onto paper for fear I should forget them, as one tries to remember and fix a dream. Even now, re-reading the May entries, I am astonished to find how much I have forgotten already, and how far we seem to have travelled since then.

Now everything seems to be clear and fixed. We are not giving in. We are just going to go on fighting. Horrible things are probably in store for us next month, but we know what they are likely to be. Nobody can let us down any more, because we are fighting alone. We know that we are not going to disgrace ourselves, whatever happens. The worst fear of all is over and done with: the fear that democracy might go down in Europe, and Freedom be surrendered, without one real blow being struck in her defence. That can't happen now, and it was the worst fear, because it struck at the roots of our faith. Hitler may win; I suppose the odds are still heavily on his side. But, please God, we'll give him such a pounding before he does that he'll never be the same man after it.

People don't look upset or strained any more. They look grim but normal. I am sure that, spiritually, we have found our feet. If Hitler means to blitz London next month I think he has left it too late.

I have heard again from my friend in Kansas. Last time she wrote she wasn't certain we would fight on. Now she is, and she is so pleased that she says perhaps we *are* a democracy. This is a lot from her. For what she means is: perhaps we do really love Liberty.

But she has shocked me to the core, and I shall write and tell her that she doesn't deserve the name of an American. Some months ago she wrote and said she could never explain to me what it is that Americans don't like about the British. I would never understand. So I wrote back and said I thought I did to some extent. Wasn't it what Meg March and John Brooke felt about Miss Kate Vaughn? So she said in a postscript to her next letter, 'I don't get the allusion to Meg March and John Brooke and Kate Vaughn. Please explain.' So I wrote back and said, as far as I can remember:

> Meg and Miss Kate were sitting beside a river, at a picnic, reading Schiller with John Brooke, their host's tutor. And Miss Kate asked Meg if she studied with her governess. And Meg said she had no governess. 'I forgot,' said Miss

Kate, patronisingly, 'young ladies in America attend school more than they do with us. Very fine schools they are too, my Papa says.' Meg made the terrible revelation that she was a governess herself. 'Oh, indeed,' said Miss Kate. Poor Meg, for the first time in her life, was made to feel she had lost caste. Good worthy John Brooke said something good and worthy about American girls liking to be independent. Whereupon Miss Kate launched into a horrible speech about how in England also there were many talented and accomplished young persons who held posts as governesses in the highest families and were scarcely despised at all 'because they are the daughters of gentlemen, you know.' Upon which Meg and John felt as you do.

I was rather pleased at being able to quote so much of it for I am sure it is nearer thirty than twenty years since I read it. But you could knock me over with a feather. My friend in Kansas now writes:

Who are Meg March, and John Brooke and Miss Kate? Are they people in a book?

Dammit! I'm a better Yank than she is. I'll never let her hear the end of this. I've a good mind to send her a cable:

LITTLE WOMEN WHERE WAS YOU RAISED.

Chapter Six

September: 'We Can Take It'

1

It has come at last.

On the nine o'clock news it said that there is the most awful raid on London. While it was still daylight some raiders got through and dropped incendiaries which took hold and caused big fires, lighting up all the sky. And now they are dropping high explosives. It seems to be the East End and the docks. But an observer on Highgate Hill said that the whole of London was a sea of flame.

This is what we have been waiting for, ever since the war began. Ever since Munich. *Ever since Guernica.*

What is happening to David?

✖

Next day. It does not sound so bad as it did last night, though bad enough. Quite a lot of London seems to be left.

And the people can take it. Every bulletin makes us more sure of that. I feel ashamed that I ever had any doubts. But indeed I never doubted their intrinsic courage. I was only afraid of the effects of shock and muddle, and that they would never get the chance to show what they are – just as our soldiers have never yet had a chance.

Now everybody will know – from China to Peru.

No letter from David today.

✖

Next day. Another frightful raid again last night. I suppose it will go on, now, night after night, without respite.

Nothing from David today. I would try to ring him up, but if every wife who has a husband in the blitz started doing that, it would block the line for urgent messages. If he was a soldier I couldn't ring him up in the middle of a battle to ask how he is getting along. I must wait, like a soldier's wife.

Nobody seems to have had any letters from London. I think if he wasn't all right I should have heard pretty promptly. So no news is good news.

The newspapers continue to come out in fine style, though they don't arrive till the late afternoon. That shows that all is not chaos in London.

✕

Next day. It goes on. The hospital where Claire's parents are has been hit. Neither was injured. Claire's mother is terribly ill still, and they are moving her to the country. I fear the shock and fatigue will be very bad for her. He has to stay behind, working among the injured.

There was a picture of the hospital in the paper, which I recognised, and I hid it, meaning to break it to Claire very gently. I thought it might upset the child to feel they had been in such danger. But the post came, and she rushed in, much excited, to proclaim:

'Dadda and Mama have been bombed!'

She did not seem to be worried at all. I don't think, even now, that they are really taking it in.

Nothing from David though Claire did get a London letter.

✕

Next day. As far as we can gather, it seems that the dead and wounded are fewer than the authorities expected and the homeless and hungry the real problem. Also the people are crowding down into any underground shelters they can find, just as Anna's friends said they would. It is maddening to think of all the suffering that might have been prevented.

The pictures in the papers make one's brain reel. But I don't have to write about that. I shall never have to try to remember what this week is being like. It is so burnt into me that I feel as if it would go on and on long after it is over. Besides it is what we expected, both the horrors and the glory.

Still nothing from David.

✕

Next day. Thank God! A whole sheaf of letters from David. He is all right. I feel ashamed to be so relieved when so many women's husbands are not all right.

Nothing very awful seems to have happened in his sector. The letter with the latest date describes the grand new barrage they have got, which seems to be a great comfort to all Londoners. He says it sounds really noble, like a pride of lions roaring round the town. It's strange they couldn't have had it to start with.

David says there is real beauty about London in the blitz. He says it thrills him when he goes on patrol, the blackout makes the houses look much grander, like precipices standing up in the moonlight, and the geometry of searchlights across the sky. And then the AA barrage is like a huge orchestra, bursting out into a deafening roar and dying down to a distant grumble. And little pygmy wardens in tin hats run about in the foreground like ants. It sounds the way the *Götterdämmerung* ought to look (and never does) on the stage.

He is on duty every other night at his post, which is under a church. The wardens go on patrol in twos, and if bombs drop they are allowed to take refuge in doorways. He says the women wardens are annoyingly brave and never want to stand in doorways, so he prefers to patrol with men.

On his off nights David sleeps in the cellar of a family hotel that belongs to my mother-in-law, who ran it herself until seven years ago. The rent provides her whole income, so I hope no bomb has its number. On quiet nights David's group of wardens take turns sleeping on mattresses among heaps of anthracite.

One of the wardens, bombed out of his sleeping place, pulled himself from the wreckage and walked along the street to get to a friend's house to ask if he could sleep there the rest of the night. In the blackout he walked into a rope stretched between two houses to stop people going up that street because the houses were unsafe. He fell over the rope and both the houses fell down. In the warden's log the entry just says, 'At 3.30 am Mr Gamble collided with two houses and demolished them.'

David went down one street where a shop window had been blown out and the street littered with wax figures. He said it was the most ghastly thing he has seen so far, all those pink wax arms and legs lying about, and simpering heads. He says no real 'corpus' could look half so sinister. He does not say if he has had much to do with real corpuses. I fear it is inevitable. But I feel he won't tell me really all about this week for a long time. Reading his letters over I find that he seems to have told me rather little.

But he is all right.

2

Hitler made a big mistake when he bombed Buck House. If he was aiming at our morale he chose the wrong targets. Buck House and Limehouse are the two places where he won't find quitters. In fact, he'd have a job to find them anywhere, as the ones we had have run away to quieter countries.

The King and Queen go round every day talking to

bombed people. Now their own house has had it they are quite a family party. As always, they are doing their job nobly. Bess is really a tip-topper. That woman can't help doing the right thing: smiles and makes little jokes when little jokes are wanted, and bursts into floods of tears when tears are the only comment. It seems she saw the ruins of a school where a lot of children had been buried. She talked to a warden who had tried to dig them out. She asked if he had got very tired.

'I didn't notice,' he said. 'It might have been your children or mine.'

Whereupon she howled unashamedly, and the women and wardens standing round, who had been wanting to howl, felt able to do so, and crowded round her to comfort her.

I don't know how she does it. Simply by being herself, I suppose: an out-and-out nice woman. Her reactions are always right because they come straight from her heart. She is just such another as little Kittenface, at Viola's boarding house. We sat quite close to them in church this spring and I had a good look at her. Along with her grace and dignity and simple good breeding, she has that look of clear innocence, that single-hearted look, which is the unique possession of out-and-out nice women.

※

An order I sent to a London shop, which was bombed this week, was executed within four days. Posts are getting back to normal. The newspapers appear regularly every day. I don't think London has been more than scratched yet.

3

I'm sure that something happened on September 15. I believe they tried some kind of invasion, after having battered at

London for a week, and that it failed. A lot of people here believe it. Here are the reasons:

1. There was a tremendous day air battle, such as we have not had for some time. It's said we shot down over 200 planes, but the official figures are 180. It was a victory on the scale of August 15.
2. The church bells, signal for invasion, were rung all over the West. The newspapers and the wireless say this is a mistake and that some fishing boats were mistaken for the German fleet in a fog. Anything you say, Mr Duff Cooper!
3. The Home Guard were called up in the middle of the night. I woke up to hear our next door neighbour backing his car stealthily out of the garage. As he drove off, another HG farther up the road was getting his car out. I leant out of the window. The night was calm and moonlit; the moon sparkled on the flat sea. And there was a subdued hum everywhere, far and near, as if hundreds of cars were on the roads and lanes.

I was so restless and excited that I got up and dressed and went out, up the road a little way into the fields. I could hear, faintly, how car after car changed gear as it went up the steep hill out of the town towards the road that runs west. There was a most extraordinary feeling in the air as if the whole country, from end to end, was alert and waiting. The very houses and trees and hedges seemed to be crouching down against the earth and listening. The night was full of rustling and whispering as if hundreds of people were talking and moving about very quietly. There were no planes. Nothing in the sky but the stable moon, unconcernedly taking her course. I kept thinking people had spoken close to me, at my elbow. But I saw nobody except a line of men slipping past a gap in a stone wall at the top of the field.

I went back to bed. Very early in the morning I heard the cars come back. Mary Keith says that none of the Home Guards are allowed to say where they went or what they did, but a friend of hers, who is a messenger, had to drive a hundred miles to somewhere in the middle of the night. She said it was like that all the way. All the Home Guards out. She was challenged at every barrier by ancient colonels waving ancient guns and was terrified lest something should go off by mistake.

Whatever it was, there is nothing about it in the news. But we are all convinced that there was some attempt to seize the West while everybody's attention was concentrated on the bombing of the East. And it's clear it must have been foiled.

✕

Nanny thinks we ought to bomb Rome. She feels passionately about it.

'Buckingham Palace is as dear to me as St Peter's Church is to Mussolini,' she says.

In vain do I tell her that even if we could get there we would have no right to bomb the Vatican City, that it is neutral and it would be as much if a crime as bombing Lisbon or Dublin or Basle.

'Just like their tricks,' she grumbles, 'to make their places neutral.'

She evidently regards the Basilica of St Peter's as Mussolini's parish church, and the Concordats as a Fascist trick. But after long argument she conceded this much:

'You mean that St Peter's and the Vatican belong to all the Roman Catholics everywhere? And it would be hard on the Roman Catholics in America and Ireland and such places to lose their Holy Place? Well, perhaps that is so.'

I let it go at that. It's near enough. Nanny's views are important and worth attending to because, upon many subjects, they are the views of great masses of our population. She does not want reprisals on civilians.

She does not want women and children to be killed. She is very strong on that. Whatever the Germans do, she says, we are not going to become butchers ourselves. Nor does she want the houses of the poor to be bombed, either in Italy or Germany. And she hopes we shall always respect hospitals and the Red Cross.

But she has not much use for the idea that we should avoid vandalism and try to leave the beautiful places in Europe intact as far as possible. She regards this as a slur on our own possessions.

'Haven't we got beautiful churches and lovely old places,' she cries, 'and aren't they being smashed up and destroyed for ever? I get tired of this idea that everything in foreign countries is so much better than poor old England, and it doesn't matter if we lose our beautiful buildings, that we have loved and reverenced for hundreds of years, so long as places like Venice are left untouched. It's all very well for you to cry up Florence and Rome, but what does that mean to all the thousands and millions of poor people who have never been there and will never be able to afford to go? Let *them* get a taste of the bitterness they are giving us. Let them feel what it is to lose something beautiful that they took a pride in.'

I try to point out that it isn't a case of *ours* and *theirs*; that beautiful things in Europe are the common heritage of Western civilisation, that she has often said herself that we must try to get a United States of Europe, and we must try to leave it as much as we can intact, for our own children to enjoy together with German and Italian children. She agrees with me, but without much enthusiasm. I think she agrees with me enough that, while she will grumblingly go on saying that Rome should be bombed, she would never loudly demand it. And I think the same holds good for vast numbers of our people.

And some of what she says is unanswerable. It is true that this common heritage has been enjoyed by far too few people, and that London's East Enders, who by their courage and sacrifice are doing most to save civilisation, have in the past enjoyed the smallest share in it. It's asking a very great deal of them to suggest that, from their point of view, the destruction of the Doge's Palace or the Medici Tombs would be any great loss. if I don't see that we can ask it unless we can offer them some sure hope for their future, some hope that it may be their children, or their grandchildren, for whose sake these things are saved.

But, as I said to Nanny, such hopes might be more quickly realised than we suppose if only we could secure a peaceful world in which the production of wealth could be carried on in a sensible way, with all countries co-operating to get general prosperity instead of economically cutting each other's throats. Travel is growing cheaper all the time. Hundreds of things are within the reach of a working-man's purse, or were till the war broke out, which he could never have dreamed of having even fifty years ago. Given peace and uninterrupted progress, the standard of life would go up and up. But Nanny's economics are sticky. She will not see that a man who gets more money is no better off than a man who, by some improvement in production, is able to buy more with the money he has got.

✖

But then I don't like Socialism. I hate the idea of batches of the proletariat shipped off at State expense on a trip to Rome. I hate the implied suggestion that it is the State's job to tell them what to think of Rome when they get there. I'd like to see all our people in good jobs, with wages sufficient to allow a fair margin for pleasure, recreation, and culture. And then let some wicked capitalist organise, at a profit to himself, trips to Rome at a price which working people could pay. I'm sure in a peaceful and progressive world it should be possible, and an incentive to even wickeder capitalists to make larger profits by providing even cheaper trips.

When Bob and his friends go on about the capitalist system I often think of Dr Johnson: 'A man is seldom more innocently employed than when he is making money.'

There is a photograph in the paper of a man with his wife and child leaving their bombed house, in a poor little street. He is turning back to take a last look at the heap of rubble which was once his home. But the woman strides proudly on, her head up, a little smile on her lips, and in her arms a small bundle of the few things they have been able to rescue.

We have a debt to them which has nothing to do with Socialism or Capitalism or any 'ism'. We must build a new home worthy of them, a London worthy of such people, as the Athenians beautified the Acropolis as a thank-offering after the Persian Wars. That has nothing to do with economics. It is a resolve which binds us all, whatever our economic theories may be. Nothing we could do for them could bear any economic proportion to the service they are rendering to civilisation. Workers get wages. But heroes and martyrs do not 'save the sum of things for pay'.

4

I've just been to tea with the Bakers, who have further light to throw on the invasion rumour last week. They have a relative who lives in a coast town about fifty miles from here. She says that on the day before (I suppose that means on the fourteenth) she was rung up by somebody who said they were speaking for the ARP. They told her that the Germans had landed and that she was to try to get to the nearest large seaport city by road if possible.

She had got the 'stay put' maxim so firmly into her head that she thought she would like further confirmation. So she rang up the police, who assured her that there was not one word of truth in the story, and said they knew there had been these telephone messages and were dealing with it.

In the afternoon a lot of women from an outlying housing estate turned up at the railway station with children and bundles, asking to be sent to the same seaport city. They said a lady in a car, with an ARP armlet, had been round telling them the same story.

Now this was exactly what the Fifth Column did in France – spreading panic and getting the people out on the roads. If the invasion was timed for the next day or night, and this trick had succeeded, troops being rushed up to stop landings might have been seriously impeded.

✕

There was very spicy gossip at the Bakers' about the identity of the lady in the car, with the armlet. Magnus, who has some claim to inside information, says we don't have to worry and that our police are not such mutton-heads as you would think. He says they often know all about somebody like that, but don't pull them in till they have found out who gives them their orders. I know a very quick way of finding that out, but I suppose we have to be civilised. If the police would arrest that woman and hand her over to me and the mothers on the beach, it would save them a lot of sleuthing, for she would tell us anything after an hour or two.

What a good thing men are more moral than women!

5

The dentist whom I visited today has some more invasion stories. He had just had a sailor patient who professed to know all about it. He says the Germans started and then we set the sea on fire by some new secret device and burnt them all up. And our destroyers attacked the ones that got away from that, and 'wove in and out like a musical ride' and sank them all.

The Keiths have heard that somebody who just arrived from France says the hospitals are full of burnt Germans, but I must say it all sounds rather like the mysterious Russians in the last war, who were seen in hundreds of different parts of England on the same day, 'with snow on their boots', coming to reinforce the Allies on the Western Front. Surely the government would let us know if there was anything in it. The Germans must know if they were burnt or not, so it wouldn't be if giving anything away. The dentist says we are being very clever: that it is much more frightening for the Germans if we say nothing at all. But it sounds too clever to be true.

Viola told me that she had met an old gentleman, who struck her as an entirely level-headed and reliable person, and he told her in strict confidence a hair-raising story. He said several thousand Germans landed by air in Gloucestershire the first week in August, and within a couple of hours they were all dead and buried. No quarter was given. They were simply massacred, thrown into a pit, and the earth shovelled over them. He professed to have seen this with his own eyes. Viola quite believed him and was shocked beyond words. Subsequently his daughter, looking much embarrassed, asked her if he had said anything about dead and buried Germans. She assured Viola that there wasn't one word of truth in it and that he has never been in Gloucestershire this summer.

He obviously believed it himself though. On just that one point he was mad. And probably he has told the tale to a lot of people who believed it and are repeating it, though his daughter does her best to go about after him correcting it.

※

Being at the dentist's reminded me of a German woman I met two years ago. She was married to an Englishman, and she told me we would certainly be conquered by Hitler because we have gas at the dentist's. Germans, she said, never have gas. They train themselves to bear pain.

'Why?' I asked.

'In order to be stronger than others.'

'And what will you do when you are stronger than others?'

'Conquer them.'

'And when you have done that will you have gas at the dentist's?'

'No, we will never become soft.'

I felt that here was a gulf that would never be bridged. To us the aim of our common life was to enjoy ourselves and have a nice time, and have everybody get a nicer time; to alleviate pain, smother out injustices and extend the pleasures of body and mind made possible by civilisation. To her it was simply to be stronger than others. Not to be strong for the purpose of getting nicer things. That was not the point. She was prepared to go without gas at the dentist's for ever. She would prefer to bear pain simply because it would enable her to inflict pain on others. The nothingness, the sterility, of this appalled me. It appalls me still as a kind of hideous parable.

The tale of destruction and suffering goes on. The raids aren't quite so severe, but every day brings news of some fresh loss to individuals or the community, and until we find an answer to the night bomber there will be no end to it. Many beautiful buildings have gone. Several of our friends have lost their homes. There is a nice schoolmaster staying at the luncheon hotel. He is here in charge of some Vackies from the Thames Estuary. He was so proud of his school, one of the new, modern Secondaries. They had just got a new science wing and gymnasium opened in May. Now they are a heap of dust.

Our London house still stands up, as far as we know. I think it is rather a protection that it is a wardens' post, as there will always be somebody there to put out incendiaries. One house in our square has already been burnt out because it was empty and nobody could get in to put out the fire before it took hold.

The plate and linen are stored, and some valuable pictures, and all our clothes are now here. But everything else is there, and I don't know where we could put the furniture if we did move it, for no place is really safe and country storage is at a premium. If a bomb gets it I think we shall be glad it didn't fall on some poor little shop that was a man's livelihood as well as his home. And we shall feel that we have joined an honourable company.

I shall mind most about my dining-room chairs. There are eight of them, eighteenth-century mahogany, and I bought them with some of our wedding present cheques at a sale in Canterbury. They came from some manor house in Kent. Five years ago I decided to turn them into a lasting memorial to myself and work the seats in *gros point*. They have nice ample seats and graceful, slender, fluted legs. I got eight designs of Chinese flowers and birds from the British Museum and got the Institute of Needlework to copy them on canvas. Two were of white pheasants among tulips. One was of herons fishing among water lilies, one of herons flying over rhododendrons, one of doves in peach blossoms, one of a magpie in plum blossoms, one of storks nesting in pine trees, and one of storks on the ground under pine trees. It took me five years to work them, and the herons were exhibited in the

Empire Needlework Exhibition in 1939. And the canvasses were all stretched and put on in July, just before we went away for the summer, and the war broke out, and we never came back, and we have never even sat on them or given one party to show them off, and if a bomb gets them they will never support the backsides of my great-great-grandchildren, as I had intended. Oh well, who cares, so long as they don't accommodate Nazi backsides?

✕

Anna tells a story of a London shelter where a very small child began to sing 'God Save the King', which it had just learnt, to keep up its spirits. It brought the house down by its version:

'Long to raid over us.'

6

Miss Levy is dead. She and all her family were killed as they sat at supper one evening. Their house had a direct hit. In the Munich Crisis she and David were the only trained wardens in our London sector. They trotted off and got trained in May, 1938, when volunteers were first called for. David explained that he had to work all day but could take night duty. He expected to work in a squad of twenty or so under a full-time head warden. On Crisis Sunday, September, 1938, the borough ARP official rang up and told him that since he was the only trained man in our sector he was head warden and that his squad consisted of Miss Levy. He was also told that he must be ready to cope with raids by Thursday and must have his post in working order within twenty-four hours. Equipment was being sent. When the equipment arrived it consisted of one dinner-bell which was to be used instead of the sirens we hadn't got.

What would have happened if the raids of 1940 had happened in 1938 simply doesn't bear thinking of. We heard afterwards that our sector was more prepared than many. I blame the Chamberlain government for not preparing more, but I never can blame them for Munich. I think Hitler could have knocked us out in a week.

The women, headed by Miss Levy, were ever so much more lively and resourceful than the men. It isn't that women are braver than men. But they are not so logical. When a man sees that nothing he does can be of the slightest use, he tends to do nothing. But a woman consoles herself by flying around doing things even if the position is quite hopeless.

Poor heroic Miss Levy! And she told me, poor darling, that she had always hated loud bangs worse than anything in the world.

7

The confusion and hardship among homeless people seem to be just what we feared. The stories of shelter conditions make one feel absolutely sick. It's incredible what people are putting up with. They take it all with a formidable good temper. Yes, I do mean formidable. People of this metal are going to get exactly what they want. But I believe they want very just and sensible things.

I look at the Gluebottoms, sitting on the sands till it is safe for them to go back to their comfortable lives. It's well for them that the shelterers are not all Communists and that there is such a strong feeling in this country for tolerance and common sense. England after the war is going to belong to the shelterers. And it won't be the England Bob wants, or the Gluebottoms' England either. It will be a land fit for human beings.

Rhianon writes that the same conditions prevail on Merseyside. The trench shelters close by her house are packed from end to end every night with people lying like sardines, their coats and shawls over their heads so they just look like lumps of old clothes. You could cut the air with a knife. She goes on duty about midnight and picks her way past family after family, the mother sometimes raising a weary head, 'like a seal', to wish her good night as she passes.

At the door stand a bunch of know-alls watching the raid and commenting on each bomb:

'Ee! Yon's a booster! Happen she went on sloom clearance' (a local name for a new housing estate). 'Ee! Theer goos t'gasworks.'

Rhianon also comments on the calm and good temper and says it almost frightens her. I know what she means. It is not quite what we expected. We thought everybody would get more excited when the real blitz began – that they would meet it with a rise of emotional temper. But that is not so. People are far more imperturbable than they were in the last war.

※

Nanny and I have made friends with a woman we saw sitting on the beach, gazing out to sea. Her dead white face and staring eyes told us that she was one of many recently come here from London, homeless. We talked to her and found she came from East London. Her whole street, where she had lived all her life, her house and all her friends' houses, gone! She seemed very lonely so we asked her for tea. She is a typical sort of woman, very, very respectable, gentle in her manner, narrow-minded but kind-hearted to any trouble she can understand, intensely housewifely with one ruling passion: 'To have things nice in the house.' You would say that everything life meant to her is gone with her little home.

As soon as she got into the house her normal self seemed to begin to reassert itself. More colour came into her cheeks, more interest to her eyes. She threw a critical glance at the tea-table and commiserated me on the cheap, ugly teaspoons. 'Oh, isn't it terrible living with other people's things? I'm sure you have everything lovely at your house in London.' A look of approval at the parquet floor which I had polished that morning, and a real glow of satisfaction when she discovered I used Ronuk. So does she. We settled to a real Gorgo and Praxinoe over floor polish. Danson, we agreed, brings up the floor beautifully, but it won't do if there are men in the house. They fall about on it. The perfect polish is that which gives a nice shine and on which husbands can be induced to remain upright. As for Shineer, it's cheap, but we say cheapness isn't everything. If you want to have things nice it always pays in the end to get the best.

She had been through an awful physical shock and had sustained a severe personal calamity. But in herself she wasn't shocked. She wasn't altered, I mean; her outlook and interests had sustained no change. She wasn't very interested in the war. She simply remarked, 'We don't want Hitler.' Nanny asked if all the people in London were standing firm in spite of all they've gone through.

'Oh, yes, all the people. Why, Hitler wants to make slaves of us. Anybody takes a pride in their house, but a slave can't take a pride in anything. Henry [her husband] says those Nazis will go to their deepest ends to make *everybody* slaves. Why, even in their own country the people are slaves. Henry says that over there the Jee-stay-po can go into anybody's house without knocking – yes, go tramping right in, they would, and *finger your things!*'

Polish her floor for the Gestapo to walk on? Not much. She would rather have no floor.

That woman makes me think of the words of the younger Pitt, always recognized as the very pattern of a cold, unemotional Englishman, when Napoleon was threatening to invade us:

> If some conqueror came to this Isle, some tyrant with his armies, none should escape. I say none. Who, of English blood, would feel the same pleasure as heretofore in the primroses of spring, the pleasant scent of summer meadows, the good fellowship of the market place? The very laughter of the children would ring with a hollow sound. We should be a different people.

Under the surface stolidity with which these horrors are being met, I feel a force generating, a resolution which is simply terrific. I believe it is going to carry us far beyond beating Hitler, and help us to undertake the tasks of reconstruction and of getting a real settlement for Europe. Excitement dies down. After the last war everybody yawned and sat back and let Europe and reconstruction look after itself. But this, whatever it is, this hidden, silent passion which is carrying us along, makes tears and cheers seem childish. Our people are not going to be tricked, or bribed, or bullied. It frightens me. Not because I think it is evil. It might turn out one of the greatest forces for good in history. But it's new: outside the scope of our imagination and experience. Unpredictable.

But I do think that such a people might be capable of working out a solution for this capital and labour business, something humane and reasonable, worked out within the framework of democracy, retaining all that is best in the past and leaving full scope to the individual and to individual enterprise.

David would say I am hallooing before we are out of the wood. We haven't begun to beat Hitler yet. We are just, and only just, stopping him from beating us.

✕

Nanny has been reading a book which she finds interesting but of which she does not altogether approve. When I told her it was published in the USA as well as here she said the Americans would not like it.

Nanny: It's very blaspheemious. Makes far too free with the name of the Lord. Americans wouldn't like that. Very strict in their notions, they are.

Me: Are they?

Nanny: Oh, yes. Look at this Prohibition. Much stricter than we are. There's a place there called Dayton where they went to law to keep them from teaching about Darwin because it's contrary to The Book.

Ellen: But what about all these gangsters, Nanny?

Nanny: Oh, they aren't Americans. Germans and Italians and Irish, they are. Immigrants.

Me: But Nanny, so are nearly all Americans. They all came over from Europe one time or another and are descended from immigrants or exiles. Mr Wilkie came from a German family and Roosevelt is a Dutch name.

Nanny: Yes, and the *good* ones became Americans. The bad ones, they didn't turn into Americans. They turned into gangsters. The people who went over there were all the people who were either too good or too bad for Europe. So their good people are stricter than ours and their bad people are more lawless.

I can't help feeling there is a germ of truth in this, odd though it sounds. It is entertaining to think of American citizenship as being like a sort of inoculation which just doesn't 'take' in the case of bad people.

Another time Nanny announced that it is much more difficult to get divorced in America than it is here. I said surely not.

'Oh, yes. They've made a law that any woman that wants to get divorced has to go and stop in a place called Reno for ever so long. Just to discourage them. It's a pity we can't have some such law. If everybody here had to go and stop in some place like Macclesfield there wouldn't be near so many divorces. Anybody wouldn't take all that trouble unless their husband was beating them black and blue.'

✕

The family hotel is no more. A bomb has wrecked the whole street and killed a lot of people. David was in the basement at the time, but is unhurt.

8

The Harkness Vackies have got very stylish bathing suits that some friend gave to Mrs Harkness. I watched the four of them come out of the sea today with my four and wondered if anyone who saw them all in bathing suits, like that, could possibly tell that they come from such different homes. My own three and Claire have that look of children who have had the best of everything ever since they were born, and before they were born, for that matter: the right diet, lots of fresh air, regular hours, immediate medical attention for any small defect, skilled dental treatment. They are tall and their bones are straight and their flesh firm; their eyes are bright and their hair is burnished and shining, and their skin has a kind of bloom, a glow on it.

After two months down here of sea air, good food, and plenty of sleep, Duncan and Sheila, the two youngest Vackies, look pretty good. But Anny and Ireen still have a sub-standard look. They have more years of overcrowding and underfeeding to recover from. They have put on weight and their cheeks are nice and pink, but they haven't quite the bloom and glow they ought to have. And the teeth of all four are simply terrible. Mrs Harkness says they crumble like chalk. It isn't a case of neglect, but their mother probably didn't get enough to eat before they were born. Poverty has set its stamp on them and you can see it at a glance.

I've said before what nice children they are, how intelligent, merry, and good-mannered. No children ever deserved a good start more, but they've had a raw deal. It worries me. I wish I could be a Socialist. I mean I wish I could believe in Socialism as an economic system and a sure remedy for these evils. Because then I wouldn't worry but would just feel: oh, it's quite simple – we've merely got to go Socialist and all will be gas and gaiters.

But I can't believe that. So now I worry because as a human being I feel that something simply must be done, and I don't know what. Children like these ought to get a better chance. From what I hear of their Mum she has done wonders in the most hopeless conditions. It worries Mrs Harkness too. She has got so fond of them; she says they must go back to something better. But when I ask what is to be done she is stumped.

Work for their Dad and a decent house is what they need. Housing we can do something about. But what about unemployment? I cannot believe that Socialism would cure it. I cannot believe that any one country can cope with it. It's a world curse. Only world measures, enlightened measures taken by all countries in concert, will get at the root of the trouble. If it doesn't pay any capitalist to employ Anny's Dad it won't pay the State. And if it doesn't pay the State we shall simply be eating our own tails if we manufacture a job for him. Get a world demand for goods and there will be a world demand for labour and there will be a job for Anny's Dad and for the poor Okies in *The Grapes of Wrath*, and for the *Arbeitslos* in *Kleiner Mann – Was Nun?* But how long will it be before all nations see that? And have Anny & Co got to go on getting a raw deal till they do? When two men go after one job wages go down.

When two jobs are waiting for one man wages go up. If you get a world demand for goods, the working people will get more pay and be able to buy more, and the demand for goods will be increased. For one nation to go Socialist is like stopping a clock in order to give oneself more time.

9

I had news in a letter today of an acquaintance who has gone to California to write poetry 'because no artist can live in Europe.'

Marry come up! It's difficult for anybody to live in Europe at the moment, but a lot of people have to. Still, I dare say he is right to go and write poetry in conditions where he can do it most efficiently – granting the assumption that his poetry is worth more to the human race than his services as a fire fighter. It doesn't much matter where he is bodily, but it does matter where he is mentally. An artist is not a reporter and he does not need a ringside seat: he does not need to be here to know what is happening here. Homer wasn't a war correspondent, and no eyewitness has painted the stable at Bethlehem. But if he thinks that there is no material for poetry here he is a blind worm. It's lying about in heaps. In fact poetry is the only medium in which the real truth can be told about life here, which is why this journal is so unsatisfactory, because I am not a poet.

A lot of pacifists have gone away for the same reason. They want to remove themselves to a purer atmosphere. If they had stayed here and told us we are wrong one could respect them. Maybe we are wrong. Perhaps we are not taking the right course to overcome evil. But if they want to say so, let them stay and share with us the terror and suffering produced by evil.

America is not necessarily a purer atmosphere. She is not a pacifist country. The great mass of her people are no more pacifist than the great mass of the people over here. They hate and loathe war as we do, and they want to keep out of it. But they do not think it is wrong for a country to defend itself when it is attacked, and if anybody attacked them they would certainly fight.

There is a good deal of bitterness about people who have 'run away'. I would not like to be them when they come back. Public opinion is so indiscriminate. I am sure some who had perfectly creditable reasons for going away will be unjustly cold-shouldered, while others who have merely thought of themselves will get away with it. Needless to say, the Gluebottoms are most indignant with anyone who has managed to be safer than they are, though what good they themselves are doing by sitting here and eating up food supplies, I don't know. It is not virtuous merely to *be* here if you aren't trying to help. We 'do our duty as we understand it' with ferocious determination – then we are in the battle. Those who merely consider their own safety are outside the battle, *wherever* they are.

David has told his mother about the family hotel. She took the blow like the game old thing she is. Even the money side of it does not worry her as much as we feared. She said, very sweetly:

'It would be much more disagreeable if we were not all so fond of one another.'

I'm afraid the poor darling has exaggerated notions as to the amount of compensation she will get. But one shock at a time. Let her build castles in the air. With her angina she may not live to see them tumble down, so why be in a hurry to disillusion her?

✕

David has been coping with a flood in the Bayswater Road, where a bomb fell on a water main. He and another warden were sent to get boats from the Serpentine, in Hyde Park, to row up and down the streets to get people out of flooded houses.

He says that he has been rather taken aback at the deliberate callousness and brutality which the younger wardens, of both sexes, assume when talking of casualties.

'We got five bods out of the pub at the corner. Or five and a half bods, to be exact.'

He commented on this to another middle-aged warden who is rather a pal of his, a nice chemist, who was very kind to him when the hotel was blitzed and lent him clothes and a razor. The chemist said they are just like young medical students in their first year, who always make a point of being tough and saying raw things about operations and post mortems. He says it is a sort of self-defence against shock when you get your first encounter with the physical horrors of life. To hear young medicals talk, you would never think they were most of them going to turn into fine, humane doctors. David said:

'What about us old fogys? Aren't we getting shocks?'

'No,' said the chemist. 'A man over thirty-five has no business to be shocked at anything.'

There is a mad lady who dresses up as a nurse and wanders round into all the wardens' posts at night. She drifted into the men's sleeping room, where those off duty take naps on mattresses, and said brightly:

'Anybody want me? I'm a certified midwife.'

10

Some more letters from the USA. They arrive in batches. I suppose they come on the same boat.

One of my American friends has sent me a little book, the journal of a woman named Dolly Sumner Lunt, who was born in the State of Maine, married a Georgia planter, was widowed, and saw Sherman's army march over her plantation, destroying property along the way. It is a poignant record, the more so because the sympathies of the writer were divided. Her heart was with the South but her reason was against slavery.

The American Civil War, which I understand the Southerners still insist upon calling the War between the States, is something that I often ponder over now. It comforts me to think of it because it is a complete answer to the slogan 'War settles nothing.' That slogan is not true. The Civil War did settle something. There was terrible suffering and destruction, but a decision was reached, and history shows it to have been a beneficial decision.

Where would America be now if the Union had not been preserved? I don't believe the first secession would have been the only one. If the principle of a right to secede had once been established, what is now the USA might well be divided into three or four nations instead of being united to preserve itself against all threats to democracy. What tremendous advantages Hitler would have gained from that! It is sad that the decision could not be reached without fighting, but the fighting did settle something important not only for the USA but for the world.

✕

There is a new note in this last batch of letters from America. They are as kind and anxious and sympathetic as ever but there is not the undertone of hopelessness there used to be. Letters written in June breathed a prayer that we, our little family, would find safety. I don't think they hoped for more than that. Now they are beginning to have hope for the country. They hardly dare say so yet, but I feel it. Of course these letters were written before the big bombings began, and I think the events since then must have strengthened that dawning hope.

My friends who write to me are all fond of England. They criticise her, of course, in various degrees of severity, but they all love things about this country and have personal friendships here. If we went down it would be a terrible shock and grief to them; they would feel they had lost something they cared for, even if it should turn out that there were no serious threats to their own safety.

I never allow myself to assume that these friends of mine are representative of the vast mass of opinion in USA. I tell myself that their sentiments may not coincide at all with the sentiments of those millions of Americans, unknown to me, who seem sometimes so near and sometimes so far away. But I can't help feeling that these September bombings, and the way our people are standing up to it, will create a liking, or the beginnings of a liking, for Britain among a lot of Americans who were indifferent or perhaps rather hostile before. Everyone likes courage. It is the most universal of virtues; nearly everyone has a great deal of it, and yet it is the most admired. Every man feels fine when he hears a story of courage, because something in his own heart tells him that he is like that too – and it tells no lie. That is why stories of courage make people feel more brotherly to one another.

This growth of sympathy, if only it can be followed up, might make a great difference in the history of the world: it might be a foundation for an understanding and cooperation after the war which would be a wonderful influence for good.

The things we care for most and the things the Americans care for most are really the same. But we must try very hard to see all this from their point of view and realise their problems.

There's a thing I always want to tell my American friends when I write, but I have never quite known how to put it, lest it might seem I was wanting to urge them to come into this war. I don't know nearly enough to know if they would be well advised to do that; it depends on hundreds of facts of which I know nothing and can't judge. But however things turn out, I do hope they realise that war is not the very worst thing that can happen to a country. It is nearly the worst, but not quite. We see that very clearly over here. I think that we are in some ways happier now than we were when we suspected that we were paying too high a price for peace. To do that is worse than war. I have wanted to say this to comfort my friends across the sea in case this awful calamity should befall them. But I haven't known how to put it without seeming to suggest that they have been paying too high a price for peace – which I don't think at all.

11

The weather has broken and we are getting those equinoctial gales we have been waiting for. For some reason they seem to think the invasion will be off for some months once the big gales start. This very tense phase is over till the turn of the year, though we have still the bombings and the sirens to shake our nerves.

The leaves are beginning to turn and today I have rinsed through and dried our bathing dresses and put them away till next year. The summer is over.

What a summer!

I was just going to write that I wouldn't have missed it for anything. But when I think how lucky we have been so far, and what others have had to suffer, I feel I have no right to say that. Some great sorrow may come to this family still. I may then earn my right to say it.

But we have certainly taken life to pieces and found out what it is made of. We have come a long, long way since we all went to church on the National Day of Prayer.

I have prayed so often since then, alone in the long nights without David, and in church with the children, and so have millions of other women prayed, and who is to say that our prayers have not been heard? Look how we have come this summer through the deep waters, through perils and hazards which all the world thought must overwhelm us. We have not reached the far shore yet, and it may not be God's will that we should I ever come there. But we have come this far, trusting in the strength we prayed for and that He has given. We must not think of Him as a Tribal God, leading us only among mankind. We don't know what prayers rise up to Him among the German people, but if they are the prayers of faith and resignation they will be answered, and He will have mercy on His people there, and lead them, as well as us, to peace and better days. We I must all pray to be delivered from the heathen: from

> ... heathen heart that puts her trust
> In reeking tube and iron shard,
> All valiant dust that builds on dust,
> And guarding calls not Thee to guard.

Biographical note

While some biographical information about Margaret Kennedy is included in the Introduction and the Notes, it was thought that it would be helpful for the reader to also include a short Biographical Note here, since Where Stands A Wingèd Sentry *is so focused on her family's lives.*

Margaret Kennedy was born in London on 23 April 1896, the eldest of the four children of Charles Moore Kennedy and his wife Elinor Marwood, who were of Northern Irish and Yorkshire stock. Her younger brother Tristram was born in 1898, and their twin siblings David and Virginia arrived in 1901. The family lived in Leaves Green in Kent, now Greater London, near Biggin Hill airport, holidaying in Cornwall in the summers. Margaret was educated by governesses to a sufficiently high standard to enter Cheltenham Ladies College in 1912, just before her sixteenth birthday. She went up to the University of Oxford in the autumn term of 1915, to read history at Somerville College. Two of her cousins were killed in the war, in 1916 and 1917; she herself was ill enough with jaundice to have to take a year out of college to recover. Her brother Tristram was killed in 1918 fighting near Jerusalem.

Margaret graduated with the equivalent of a second-class degree in history in 1919 (the year before women were allowed to take their degrees at Oxford), and was immediately commissioned to write *A Century of Revolution* for Methuen: it was published in 1922, and was not much noticed. In 1923 her first novel was published, *The Ladies of Lyndon*, which also received little attention. While she was working on this book she had gone to Pertisau on Achensee in the Austrian Tyrol to stay with friends, and discovered a passion for mountains and walking. It also gave her a setting for her next novel, *The Constant Nymph* (1924), and she returned to Pertisau to finish the novel.

The Constant Nymph received an unstoppable swell of approval, and Margaret received congratulations from the leading literary figures of the day, including Thomas Hardy, George Moore, A E Housman and Arnold Bennett. She began to meet more people working in and around literature, and at one of the parties she attended she met her future husband, David Davies, a barrister and a former secretary to Lord Asquith, the former prime minister. They married in July 1925. A year later Margaret began adapting *The Constant Nymph*, by now a best-seller, for the stage with Basil Dean, first starring Noel Coward, and then John Gielgud as the composer Lewis Dodd.

In 1927 the Davies family moved to 27 Campden Hill Square, between Holland Park and Kensington Gardens in west London. Margaret continued to write novels and plays, while producing children of her own: Julia was born in 1928, and Sarah (Sally) in 1920. James arrived in 1935. In the late 1920s the family rented Hendre Hall, a large house in Llwyngwril near Barmouth on the North Wales coast, which became their holiday home for many years.

In 1937 David Davies became a County Court judge. Margaret had become a leading literary figure, enjoying friendships with actors and writers, who included Elizabeth Bowen, Lady Cynthia Asquith, Charles Morgan, Hilda Vaughan, Elizabeth Jenkins, Lettice Cooper, Phyllis Bentley, Marghanita Laski, Rose Macaulay and L P Hartley. While experiencing increasing anxiety over the approach of war, and concern for the safety of her friends in Germany and Austria, Margaret had to struggle at home with antagonism among her domestic staff and with running two houses, as well as her writing.

With the approach of war Margaret organised their London home into the local sector's Air Raid station. Her health began to respond to emotional stress, which brought on lumbago, and then in early 1939 she was afflicted with Bells' Palsy which gave her face the appearance of having suffered a stroke. In 1940 she contracted shingles. Meanwhile David Davies' new role as a volunteer Air Raid

Warden required him to live in London full-time, making North Wales inconveniently distant for the family to live in for the war. By the middle of 1940 the family had left Hendre Hall for a brief stay in Surrey. They moved to Sir Adrian and Lady Boult's house, Quaker's Orchard near Peaslake, a village outside Dorking. (Anne Boult was Julia's godmother.) Sir Adrian was Director of Music at the BBC and conductor of its symphony orchestra, and as his department had been moved to Bristol the house was empty. The Davies family stayed at Quaker's Orchard for only around six weeks before Margaret and the children moved to St Ives with Nanny, while David remained in London.

Margaret visited London frequently for committees and to see her husband, and eventually moved her children and Nanny out of their rented home into a hotel, which made her housekeeping much easier. In 1943 she and the children and Nanny left Cornwall, for James to go to prep school and the girls to go to Oxford High School. In July 1944 their London house was completely destroyed by a VI flying bomb. They moved into a new home a few streets away, at 11 Argyll Road, where the family stayed for fourteen years.

In 1947 Margaret visited the USA for the first time, and began writing a new cycle of novels, and an acclaimed biography of Jane Austen. More novels and critical writing followed, accompanied by increasing deafness. David Davies was knighted in 1952. His death in 1964 was a great blow to Margaret. Her health continued to deteriorate, and she died in 1967 aged seventy-one.

(See Violet Powell, *The Constant Novelist. A Study of Margaret Kennedy, 1896–1967*, William Heinemann 1983; *Orlando. Women's Writing In The British Isles From The Beginning To The Present*, http://orlando. cambridge.org; information supplied by Margaret Kennedy's family.)

Notes on the Text

BY KATE MACDONALD

Page numbers given in these notes refer to references in Violet Powell, *The Constant Novelist. A Study of Margaret Kennedy, 1896–1967* (William Heinemann, 1983). Where personal information has been supplied by Margaret Kennedy's family this is also noted.

My soul, there is a country: These lyrics were composed by the Welsh poet Henry Vaughan in the seventeenth century, but are not among his commonly anthologised works. The words took on new significance as a response to the First World War, when the English composer Charles Hubert Parry set them to music as the first in his six choral pieces, *Songs of Farewell* (1916). The resulting anthem has been collected subsequently in many church hymnals and choral collections, and would have been more familiar to Kennedy's generation as a hymn than as the original poem.

Foreword

collapse of France: after the success of the German advance on France through Belgium in May and June 1940, France and Germany signed an armistice on 22 June, giving Germany control of the French ports and an occupation zone in north and west France.

The vacillating, inconsistent good: lines 157–161 from Book IV: Despondency Corrected, of William Wordsworth's poem *The Excursion* (1814).

Dark Tower: Robert Browning's 1855 poem 'Childe Roland to the Dark Tower Came' describes a forbidding landscape of decay and despair, through which the knight has to travel to reach the Dark Tower and challenge whatever may lie within.

Lease-Lend Bill: The Lend-Lease policy was signed by President Roosevelt on 11 March 1941 to enable supplies of food, fuel and other necessary items to be sent from the USA to the UK and other Allied countries.

Wilkie: Wendell Lewis Wilkie was the Republican nominee for the 1940 US Presidential election, and favoured a more interventionist approach to the war in Europe than the winner, Franklin Roosevelt.

Julian Street: see p xix.

Chapter One

Waterloo: The Battle of Waterloo in 1815 was the climactic battle of allied forces including Britain against Napoleon Bonaparte and the French army. An invasion of England by Bonaparte had been expected since the 1790s, and this belief heavily influenced the refortification of the English coastline with forts and other defensive structures.

Armada: Philip II of Spain sent a great navy of 130 ships to invade England in 1588, and warnings of its approach were sent by fire beacons around the coast of Britain. It was defeated and wrecked by a combination of bad weather, English fireships and poor leadership.

our army in Flanders: the rapid invasion of the Netherlands, Belgium and Luxembourg by Germany during May 1940 left the French command convinced that France would be next to fall. They were unable to give the British Expeditionary Forces (BEF) any orders to advance or fall back, thus leaving the British forces trapped on a thinning line of French territory between the German advance and the Channel.

our household: In 1940 Margaret's children were Julia aged twelve, Sarah (Sally) aged ten and James aged five. Mrs Julia Davies, Margaret's mother-in-law, did indeed suffer from a heart complaint, but survived the war (166). Clemence Browne, daughter of the Australian novelist Helen de Guerry Simpson and her surgeon husband Denis Browne, was in Margaret's charge for the early years of the war while her mother was seriously ill (171). The Davies family attended Clemence's wedding in 1951 (see photograph facing 129).

sixpences: small silver coins and tokens were traditionally put into the Christmas pudding, to bring luck for the following year to the person who found them in their portion.

Chamberlain: the British government was led at this time by Neville Chamberlain, who had negotiated peace with Hitler in 1938.

Gamelin, Weygand: Commander-in-Chief of the French armed forces at the beginning of the Second World War, Maurice Gamelin commanded the French army and its allies during the German invasion with methods learned during the First World War, and is widely held to have been a disastrous leader. When Gamelin was dismissed, Maxime Weygand, then commander-in-chief of the French forces in the Middle East, was recalled to command in France. He later advocated signing the armistice with Hitler.

Chapter Two

piquet: a two-person card game.

bedding out: planting flowering plants which have been grown from seed or cuttings in a nursery, to supply instant colour to rejuvenate a flower border.

last trump: the angels' flourish of trumpets that will awaken and raise the dead on the Day of Judgement.

British Legion: the association of former British military servicemen and women, who at the time of this story would have all served during the First World War, the youngest of whom would have been in their forties.

Poland: in October 1939 Germany and Soviet Russia took control of Poland.

Manual for Mothers: *Studies in Child Development. A Manual for Mothers and Mothers' Clubs*, by Julia Clarke Hallam, had been first published in 1913.

Penrod: a collection of sketches about the adventures of an eleven year old boy in the mid-west of the US, in the years before the First World War. They might be analogous to the British *Just William* stories by Richmal Crompton.

Belgium is out: after 18 days of severe fighting the Germans had invaded Belgium and destroyed its roads and railways to such an extent that the King of the Belgians, also the Belgian army's commander-in-chief, Leopold III, requested an armistice on 27 May 1940. The Belgian government removed itself to France, and later London, as the only legitimate representative of Belgium among the Allies. Leopold and his mother Queen Elisabeth remained in Belgium in self-imposed captivity for the duration of the war.

his father: Leopold's father, Albert I, is widely regarded as a hero for his leadership and heroic conduct throughout the First World War.

Holmbury Hill: the site of an Iron Age hill fort in Surrey, with panoramic views south. It lies close to Peaslake, near where the Davies family were living for six weeks in mid-1940. (Information from Margaret Kennedy's family.)

black curtains: blackout regulations had been enforced since 1 September 1939, to prevent enemy planes being able to navigate at night by identifying population centres. Air Raid Precautions (ARP) wardens enforced these locally, and those who broke the law would be fined.

Fifth Column: the popular name for enemy spies, acting secretly within a population or military unit as a 'column' of the enemy's forces.

Dachau: a Nazi concentration camp north-west of Munich, which had been operating as a political prison for German nationals since 1933.

Oppenheim novel: E Philips Oppenheim was one of the leading authors of early thrillers and spy mysteries, selling millions of copies worldwide.

Hast mich in eine bessere Welt: Possibly a quotation from the song by Franz Schubert, 'An die Musik', 'Hast mich in eine bessere Welt entrückt', 'You have brought me to a better world'.

Guernica: in 1937 the Basque town of Guernica was bombed by the German *Luftwaffe* for the Spanish Nationalist forces under General Franco in the Spanish Civil War. Hundreds of civilians died.

Hoare-Laval plan: a secret plan between the governments of Britain and France to bring the Second Abyssinian War to an end, by giving the aggressor, Italy, half of the Ethiopian territory Mussolini was seeking to annex. When the plan became public there was a hostile reaction, and Hoare lost his post as Foreign Secretary in the British government.

hawthorn: hawthorn flowers are creamy white and blossom after the leaves have appeared on its branches.

clotted cream: a particularly thick version of cream, produced mainly in Devon and Cornwall, where the cream is stiff enough to not drip or pour, but must be spooned out of the bowl onto the scone, before or after the jam.

Cosmo Cantuar: Cosmo Lang was Archbishop of Canterbury from 1928 to 1942, and had supported the Chamberlain government's appeasement policy towards Hitler. 'Cantuar' is an abbreviation of Cantuariensis, Latin for Canterbury, the traditional signature of the Archbishop.

Sennacherib: king of the Assyrian Empire, notorious for his Biblical role as the destroyer of Babylon and his attack on Jerusalem. Byron depicted him most famously as a wolf who came down on the fold in his 1815 poem *The Destruction of Sennacherib*.

Arnold Bennett: prolific and influential English novelist, critic and literary arbiter. He had died in 1931.

T: Tristam Kennedy, the elder of Margaret's two brothers, had died fighting near Jerusalem in 1918 (39).

our hope for years to come: from the hymn 'O God Our Help In Ages Past', by Isaac Watts (1708), altered by John Wesley thirty years later. It is commonly sung on solemn national or state occasions in Britain.

that grey November morning: on 11 November 1918, the Armistice was formally announced at 11.00am, and was widely expected.

Rhianon: Eluned Lloyd was Margaret's close friend at Oxford (40). Both names are distinctively Welsh.

Time, like an ever-rolling stream: a quotation from 'O God Our Help In Ages Past'.

an honest man's the noblest work of God: from Epistle 4 of *An Essay on Man* (1733) by Alexander Pope, or from 'The Cotter's Saturday Night' by Robert Burns (1786).

an honest God's the noblest work of man: from *The Gods* (1876) by the American agnostic Robert G Ingersoll.

Porthmerryn: St Ives, a fishing town and an artists' settlement on the north coast of Cornwall, where Margaret had stayed for many holidays as a child (172).

Dunkirk: the evacuation of the Allied forces from the coast at Dunkirk, under heavy German bombardment, took place between 26 May and 4 June 1940.

If you have it: a quotation from J M Barrie's play *What Every Woman Knows* (1908): 'It's a sort of bloom on a woman. If you have it, you don't need to have anything else; and if you don't have it, it doesn't much matter what else you have.'

Munich Crisis: the Munich Agreement was signed on 30 September 1938 between Germany, Britain, France and Italy, to allow Nazi Germany to annex the Sudetenland territory of Czechoslovakia, inhabited largely by German speakers. The agreement was celebrated at the time for preventing war in Europe, but is now regarded as an act of appeasement, which Hitler had no intention of abiding by. However the time it gained did allow rearmament to speed up in the Allied countries opposed to Nazi Germany's territorial ambitions.

genial current of the soul: from Thomas Gray's *Elegy Written In A Country Churchyard* (1742–50).

Géle: as we find out later, she meant General de Gaulle, who had been lobbying for the French army to adopt armoured infantry divisions for many years.

Reynaud: Paul Reynaud, French politician who opposed the Munich agreement, and succeeded Daladier as Prime Minister of France in 1940. He refused to support an armistice with Germany and was arrested by Pétain's Vichy administration on trying to escape from France after the German invasion: he spent the rest of the war in prison.

the Tyrol and the Salzkammergut: much of *The Constant Nymph* was drawn from Margaret's stay in the Austrian village of Pertisau, on Achensee (47) in the Tyrol. The Salzkammergut is a mountain region east of Salzburg.

Maginot Line: a line of concrete forts and military battlements built by France in the 1930s to prevent a land invasion of France. In the event Germany invaded France by going round the north end of the Line through the Low Countries.

Trop tard. C'est fini. Nous sommes trahis: Fr, 'It's too late. It's over. We've been betrayed.'

the test of democracy is public virtue: possibly paraphrasing Montesquieu in *De l'Esprit des lois* (*The Spirit of Law*, 1748), in which he says that a necessary condition for the existence of a republican government is that the people holding power must possess public virtue, in that they desire to achieve public good.

Bien sûr, on sait là-bas que l'un sans l'autre est foutu: Fr, 'Of course, we all know that one without the other is stuffed.'

Halifax: Lord Halifax was a British politician and diplomat, and served as Foreign Secretary from 1938 to 1940. He helped to create the British policy of appeasement.

Cordell Hull: the US Secretary of State from 1933 to 1944, who received the Nobel Peace Prize in 1945 for his work in establishing the United Nations.

France At War: published in Britain in 1940 by Heinemann.

dishonoured graves: possibly a reference to Tennyson's poem 'Come not, when I am dead, / To drop thy foolish tears upon my grave' (1853).

the Nightmare Life-in-Death that thicks man's blood with cold: from Coleridge's *The Rime of the Ancient Mariner* (1797), in which Death and Life-in-Death dice for the ship's crew's souls, and the latter, a living corpse, wins.

Polly: *Polly*, an opera by John Gay, was the sequel to his *The Beggar's Opera* (1728). It was banned from public performance in Gay's lifetime, and its first official performance was not until 1777, but it had already been swiftly pirated and sold illicitly in printed form from 1729.

Axis: the military alliance of Germany, Italy and Japan in the Second World War.

Welsh gypsies: despite the implication that the Davies family have been long settled in their Surrey home, they had in fact only been living there for a few weeks (information from Margaret Kennedy's family). For many years the family's country home had been in North Wales, but this had become too far away from London and David Davies's work.

Gin and Italian: recipes vary as to the correct quantities for a Gin and It(alian), which is made from gin, sweet Italian vermouth and a dash of bitters.

the moon set and the Pleiades: a quotation from J A Symonds' translation *The Poems of Sappho* (1883), which reads 'The moon has set, and the Pleiades; it is midnight, the time is going by and I recline alone'.

Leonidas: Leonidas was a king of Sparta who died in command of the pass at Thermopylae with a small number of allied forces, holding back the huge Persian invading forces.

Chapter Three

offered me a bed: while Margaret, the children and Nanny did initially rent a small house in St Ives, they soon moved into 'the annexe of a local hotel' (173).

Winston: Winston Churchill, British Prime Minister from May 1940.

live on their own humps: like the camel.

À bas les Anglais, Vive les Boches: Fr, 'Down with the English', 'Long live the Germans'.

'Eh, doctor': Scots, 'Doctor, you shouldn't waste such fine words on people like us. We'd very much like to know how things are with our child, and maybe Sister will let us know. You see, we don't understand you.'

'Well, wumman': Scots, 'Well, ma'am ... we've taken everything out of his stomach that shouldn't be there.'

Bernhardt: the great nineteenth-century French classical actress Sarah Bernhardt performed the title role in Racine's play *Phèdre* (1677) many times, as it was one of her signature roles.

Lafayette: Gilbert du Motier, Marquis de Lafayette, fought in the American War of Independence (1775–83) by which the American colonies wished to separate from British rule under George III, and he became an American hero.

**'*Que voulez-vous? C'est la guerre'*: Fr, 'What do you expect? It's war.'

courants d'air: Fr, 'draughts', or chilly currents of air.

Dalladeer: Édouard Daladier was Prime Minister of France and a signatory to the 1938 Munich Agreement.

were very ill: Sarah Davies had been a delicate child, and Margaret and her husband moved their bedroom to the nursery floor so that Nanny and the children could have the larger rooms downstairs which were more convenient for nursing the baby. They only regained their bedroom eight years later, to Nanny's disgust (87).

George and Bess: King George VI and Queen Elizabeth. Bess is a more upper-class abbreviation for Elizabeth than 'Betty' or 'Lizzy' would have been at this period. Its use doesn't suggest intimacy but approval.

Rhianon: Eluned Lloyd's husband Garmon Jones had died unexpectedly in 1937; they were childless.

Anderson huts: Anderson shelters were inexpensive DIY air raid shelters designed in 1938 and named after Sir John Anderson who had led British air raid precaution preparations. They could be embedded in the garden and covered with earth for planting, or erected at ground level, and would have a very good record in protecting their inhabitants during air raids.

Vernon Bartlett: a Member of Parliament opposed to appeasement, and also the diplomatic correspondent of the *News Chronicle*, a liberal daily paper.

Pétain: at the end of the First World War Philippe Pétain had been Marshall of France, its highest-ranking general. He orchestrated the agreement with Germany in 1940 that ended the Battle for France, and set up the collaborationist Vichy government of occupied France. After the war he was tried for treason, but due to his advanced age and First World War service was spared the death penalty, dying in prison.

Mandel: Georges Mandel, formerly Rothschild, was a French politician vehemently opposed to an armistice with Germany in 1940, or to work in the Vichy government. He became a French Resistance leader and died in 1944.

jusqu'au boutist: Fr, one who will not give up until the end.

Devil take the hindmost: Scots proverb meaning that the last one will have the worst fate.

Abbess: abyss.

I *see*, not *feel*, how beautiful they are: from Coleridge's *Dejection. A Ode* (1802), on seeing the stars at night.

Nature never did betray: from Wordsworth's *Lines (Composed a Few miles Above Tintern Abbey ... 1798)*, 'Knowing that Nature never did betray / The heart that loved her'.

It Can't Happen Here: a satirical novel published in 1935 by the American novelist Sinclair Lewis, describing the rise to totalitarian power of a fascist US President.

The Grapes of Wrath: the great American novel of the Great Depression, in which farming families try to find work on the west coast.

Willa Cather, Dorothy Canfield: a former magazine journalist and editor, Willa Cather's fiction celebrated the endurance of the immigrant settling in North American frontier country, and its magnificent natural landscapes. Dorothy Canfield Fisher was an American social reformer whose fiction advocated strongly for women's rights and racial justice. She was also a prominent literary leader, shaping the nation's taste through the Book of the Month Club from 1921 to 1951.

De Gaulle: after the fall of France General De Gaulle would lead the Free French forces against Nazi Germany from his base in London.

Quisling: someone who cooperates with an invading force to gain power, after a Norwegian wartime leader who collaborated with the invading Nazi forces in Norway.

Rich with the spoils of Time: in Gray's *Elegy Written In A Country Churchyard* (1742–50) Knowledge had the ample page.

Ringworm, pinkeye, itch, scab, and impetigo: ringworm is a fungal infection of the skin; pinkeye is conjunctivitis, an inflammation of the outer membrane of the eye and inner eyelid; impetigo is a bacterial infection of the skin. Itch and scab are symptoms of all or some of these, and all are indicators of poor hygiene and diet.

Lysol: a strong disinfectant with hydrogen peroxide as its active ingredient, used for cleaning clothes and household surfaces.

Chapter Four

Tabouis: Geneviève Tabouis was a leading French journalist with strong anti-fascist and pro-Republican views, whose correct predictions in her reporting gave her the justifiable reputation of deep knowledge of interwar international politics. She escaped France in 1940 and worked as a journalist and commentator from New York.

Eire: Ireland maintained neutrality during the Second World War, due to memories of the Anglo-Irish Civil War in the 1920s, and antagonism to English colonialism in earlier centuries. It was also unprepared militarily for participation internationally in war. However, Ireland cooperated in many ways with the Allies behind the scenes, including sharing intelligence and interning crashed or shipwrecked Axis servicemen.

de Valera: Eamonn de Valera was serving as the Irish head of state during the war, and had been a leading politician in the War of Independence. He was involved with the Gaelic Revival, which promoted Irish culture and language.

Brian Boru: an eleventh-century High King of Ireland.

croquet: a garden game played with long mallets to hit balls through hoops. In *Alice*, the game is played with flamingos as the mallets, and the hoops are the card men, who run away once played, thus confusing the game utterly.

Sarah: in the Old Testament Sarah was the wife of Abraham, and conceived her first child in her nineties (Genesis 17.16).

The Magic Shop: a story by H G Wells first published in the *Strand* magazine in 1903.

experiment in time: from the very well-known book from 1927, *An Experiment With Time*, by J W Dunne, on precognition and a serial theory of time.

stirrup pump: a portable pump placed in a bucket of water, used to extinguish or control fires, with the bucket being replenished as needed.

fertile: futile.

tannic acid: tannic acid jelly, sold in tubes, had been an effective treatment for severe burns since the 1920s.

Oran: a large port on the Algerian coast. The attack on nearby Mers el-Kébir on 3 July 1940 was carried out by the British navy to neutralise French naval ships and prevent them being used against the Allies by Germany. 1297 French servicemen were killed.

Boule de Suif: a short story by Guy de Maupassant from 1880, also made into a film in 1934, in which a party of French citizens travel from Rouen to Le Havre by coach, fleeing the German occupation in the Franco-Prussian War. At the end of the story the prostitute in the party has finally given in and slept with the German officer who bars their passage, but then the other passengers, who have persuaded her to do this so they can all escape, reject her. The *Marseillaise* is whistled to taunt those who have abandoned French rights to dignity.

Non magnis opibus iucunde corpora curant: from Lucretius' *De Rerum*, 'people restore their bodies pleasantly enough using few resources'.

The Happy Warrior: the subject of the poem 'Character of the Happy Warrior' by Wordsworth (1807), which presents the ideal soldier in the period of the Napoleonic Wars.

Hector: eldest son of the King of Troy in *The Iliad*, killed in battle by Achilles.

the fretful porcupine: 'And each particular hair to stand on end / Like quills upon the fretful porpentine', *Hamlet* 1.5.13. An early name for a porcupine was porpentine.

Freud knows why: the psychoanalytic theories of Sigmund Freud lent themselves easily to spoofing, by inviting serious consideration of a bathetic object, like boots, as being psychologically significant.

Town Crier: an officer of a local authority employed to make public announcements, now superseded in all practical ways by modern media communications, but still retained for nostalgic and ceremonial purposes by some town councils. Such officers often wear a version of eighteenth-century uniform, with a frock coat, black cocked hat and gold lace.

go bail: must promise.

adenoidy, dowdy survivals: uncomplimentary term for the British upper classes, of whom caricatures with speech impediments (such as occurred when the adenoids grew so enlarged they affected speech), and a uniform of elderly, well-worn tweeds, were popular in the mass media.

Low: David Low was a self-taught New Zealand cartoonist whose work in Britain from the 1920s in caricaturing political figures made him famous.

splits: a particular kind of Cornish bun, made from a soft round sweet bread roll sliced open and filled with jam and cream.

Iss fay: Cornish dialect for 'Yes indeed' ('fay' being an abbreviation for 'faith', 'I' faith').

kraals: Afrikaans word for a cattle enclosure, often extended to mean a village since cattle were the basis for southern African economies before colonialism. Probably used here to suggest London as an area of many different tribes.

Stanley Baldwin: Prime Minister during the constitutional crisis leading up to the abdication of Edward VIII.

At the Circus: released in 1939.

Laugh – but smile no more: the last line of 'The Haunted Palace' by Edgar Allen Poe (1845).

Austerlitz, the *Chaconne*, the Sistine Chapel: the Battle of Austerlitz in 1805, the Ciaccona by Johann Sebastian Bach (BWV 1004, 1717–1720) and the Sistine Chapel's ceiling by Michaelangelo (1508–1512) were three major accomplishments in, respectively, military tactics, musical composition and art.

Negroes: Kennedy does not use 'Negroes', 'coloured' and 'the Jew' with the intention of being offensive, but because this was the terminology of her day.

I am a stranger with Thee: from Psalm 24, 6.12.

Blue Books: an official report from the UK government or Privy Council.

trimmers: name given to those who change their political allegiance in ways designed to do them most good, from the sailing analogy of trimming or reducing the sails to make the best use of the wind.

Paris vaut une Messe: in 1593 Henry IV of France is said to have remarked 'Paris vaut bien une Messe' (Paris is well worth a Mass) on deciding to convert to Catholicism and thus secure his hold on the French throne.

Chapter Five

twitched her mantle blue: from the last lines of Milton's poem *Lycidas* (1637), 'At last he rose, and twitched his mantle blue: / Tomorrow to fresh woods and pastures new.'

this demi-Paradise, this other Eden: from John of Gaunt's speech in Shakespeare's *Richard II*, 'This other Eden, demi-Paradise, / This fortress built by Nature for herself' (1595, 2.1.40).

College: Somerville.

Yahoos: from Jonathan Swift's novel *Gulliver's Travels* (1726), in which the Yahoos are a race of primitive creatures who have limited and superficial interests.

dam: the female parent of an animal, correlating to 'sire'. Used here facetiously in the husbandry sense.

Buck House: slang name for Buckingham Palace, the London residence of the reigning monarch.

air battle: the Battle of Britain began on 10 July 1940.

stands in the pass: see Leonidas (above).

horn-rimmed spectacles: Kennedy jokes that Communists are more likely than not to be middle-class intellectuals who can afford to get their eyes tested and wear fashionable glasses.

Gorgo and Praxinoe: characters in Theocritus's Latin poems of urban life, who chatter incessantly.

AA guns: anti-aircraft guns, fired from the ground.

sleeping together: sharing the same bed.

caught it: bore the full force of her irritation.

the whole world was in a state of chassis: from *Juno and the Paycock* by Sean O'Casey (1924).

Little Women: a hugely popular novel by Louisa May Alcott (1868–69), one of the classic works of American literature particularly beloved by American women.

Chapter Six

Götterdämmerung: The Twilight of the Gods, or Ragnarok, the last of Wagner's four dramas in the Ring Cycle.

family hotel: Margaret Kennedy's mother in law, Mrs Julia Davies was the part-owner of the Kensington Gardens Hotel, Lancaster Gate, from around 1904 to around 1939 (information from Margaret Kennedy's family). Violet Powell notes that David Davies slept in his mother's flat which she was not using (169).

Limehouse: a deprived and over-crowded district in the East End of London, diametrically opposite to Buckingham Palace in almost every respect.

howl: euphemism for weeping, which focuses attention on its sounds and veers away from acknowledging the expression of emotion, very typical of middle-class English writing at this time since the term probably derives from boarding school or university slang.

September 15: the climactic air battle in the Battle of Britain, involving 1500 aircraft, after which Hitler gave up on plans to invade Britain.

Duff Cooper: politician who served as Minister of Information in Winston Churchill's War Cabinet.

Concordats: the diplomatic agreements between the Holy See in the Vatican and sovereign states on the jurisdiction of matters that concern them both.

save the sum of things for pay: from A E Housman's poem 'Epitaph on an Army of Mercenaries' (1922); 'What God abandoned, these defended, / And saved the sum of things for pay'.

our London house: the Davies family lived at 27 Campden Hill Square, which survived until it was destroyed by a direct hit by a V1 flying bomb on 24 July 1944.

cut the air with a knife: the smell of the air was so pungent that it was almost solid.

Kleiner Mann – Was Nun: a 1932 novel by Hans Fallada, published in English as *Little Man – What Now?*, about the Depression years in Germany.

Marry come up!: a Shakespearean phrase conveying impatience, surprise or shock.

Dolly Sumner Lunt: see page xix in the Introduction.

heathen heart that puts her trust: from Rudyard Kipling's 'Recessional', a hymn composed in 1987 for Queen Victoria's Golden Jubilee.